Power Prompts

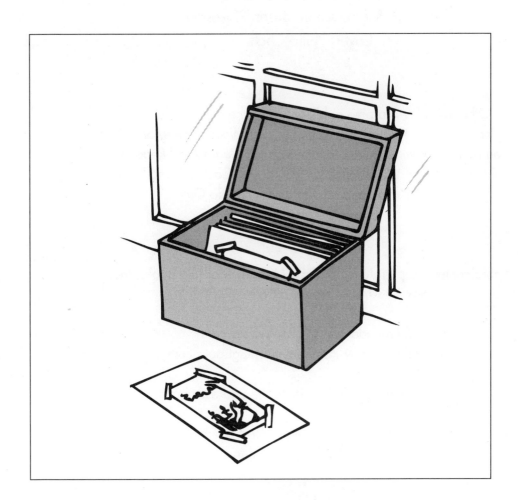

By
Murray Suid
and Wanda Lincoln

Illustrated by Philip Chalk

This book is for
Anna Mei

Publisher: Roberta Suid
Copy Editor: Carol Whiteley
Design & Production: Susan Pinkerton
Cover: Philip Chalk

Other Monday Morning publications by the authors include:
How to Teach Writing Without Going Crazy, Ten-Minute Editing Skill Builders,
Ten-Minute Grammar Grabbers, Ten-Minute Real World Reading,
Ten-Minute Real World Writing, Storybooks Teach Writing, and
The Kids' How to Do (Almost) Everything Guide.

Entire contents copyright © 1999 by Monday Morning Books, Inc.
Box 1680, Palo Alto, California 94302

Online address: MMBooks@aol.com
Web address: www.mondaymorningbooks.com

For a complete catalog, write to the address above.

"Monday Morning" is a registered trademark of
Monday Morning Books, Inc.

Dramatic Touchdown by Tim Keown ©1999 by *San Francisco Chronicle*
reprinted by permission.

ISBN 1-57612-071-6

Printed in the United States of America
987654321

Contents

Introduction

Practice!

That is the secret to writing well. Successful essayists, poets, novelists, journalists, science writers, playwrights, historians, and other word experts write a great deal, and write often. Practice does not make perfect, but it does develop the skills, knowledge, and confidence needed to write clear, correct, and creative manuscripts.

Practice That Counts

Of course, there is more to mastery than mere repetition. The practice must focus on key processes that come into play in all forms. Whether students write science reports or science fiction, business letters or haiku, they need to know how to handle such basics as:

- comparing
- condensing
- contrasting
- describing
- elaborating

- explaining
- giving examples
- interpreting
- linking ideas
- paraphrasing

- persuading
- simplifying
- speculating
- summarizing
- using humor

If students spent hours a day writing essays, stories, plays, and other works, they would naturally make progress with these skills. However, with so many other demands on their time, most students do not get sufficient practice.

That's where *Power Prompts* can help. Like scales practiced by musicians, and warm-up drills practiced by athletes, these exercises provide intense, focused experiences that move students quickly and efficiently toward mastery. Because the prompt practices are short, there is time for repetition.

Using the Materials

Power Prompts covers more than three dozen skills. Each lesson begins with a reproducible *introductory prompt*, which includes a model, an assignment, and hints for completing the exercise successfully. You can use this page to lead the class in a whole-group practice. Or students can use it independently.

Most of the exercises ask students to apply the technique in a short essay, story, or report. You will find detailed instructions for introducing or reviewing these forms in this book's Classroom Management section. With each introductory lesson, you'll find follow-up prompts designed as activity cards, usually three to six per page. You can duplicate these pages, cut out the prompts, and attach them to index cards. (A few prompts fill an entire page and might be used as bulletin board prompts.) You might pass out these cards at a set practice time, or store them in a box where students can use them for independent writing practice. (See the Classroom Management section of this book for detailed hints on setting up an Independent Writing Center.)

For more teacher-directed practice, you'll find a set of Activity Extensions in the Classroom Management section. These enrichment ideas include using video and other media.

Where to Start
There is no one right sequence for practicing the fundamentals of writing. For example, experimenting with descriptive writing does not necessarily come before practicing the three points of view. For this reason, the prompts are presented in alphabetical order. This arrangement will make it easier for you to quickly find the skill you wish to work on.

Because the sequence of practices is arbitrary, you could start with the first lesson "Comparing and Contrasting," or choose lessons that relate to your district's curriculum, or begin with lessons that address problems in your students' writing. Another option is to pick lessons that interest you. (Your enthusiasm will be a powerful motivator for students.)

Whatever sequence you use, to help you keep track of student work, we have included a Practice Log in the Classroom Management section. If you duplicate a copy for each student, the students can then take the responsibility for tracking the skills they have practiced. The Log might be kept in a notebook devoted to the *Power Prompt* practices.

Applying the Practices
The only valid purpose for practicing techniques such as descriptive writing and personification is to use them in real assignments. Thus, when you ask students to write stories, essays, plays, poems, and other works, remind them of the practices they have done. This is especially important when they reach the editing step of the writing process. The Classroom Management section includes specific tips for editing and evaluation.

We wish you great success with *Power Prompts* and welcome your comments and questions.

Murray Suid and Wanda Lincoln

Comparing and Contrasting

Writers often need to compare two subjects, explaining how they are alike and different. This technique is used in many types of writing. For example, in a story, you might compare the hero and the villain. In a science report, you might tell how two creatures—for example, ants and bees—are similar and dissimilar.

Model

A Hand Is Not a Foot

In some ways, the hand and the foot are similar. But there are also important differences.

Both the hand and the foot come as pairs. The left hand mirrors the right hand, and the left foot mirrors the right foot. Also, both the hand and the foot have main sections to which are attached five movable parts (digits). The top end of each digit is covered with a nail—a hard protective covering.

The hand's movable parts are the "fingers." One of the fingers, known as the thumb, is noticeably thicker than the other four, and is located to one side of the palm. The thumb's position allows it to make contact with each of the other four fingers. For this reason, the human thumb is called an "opposable thumb." It enables the hand to grip and manipulate things, an ability that experts believe contributed to the development of civilization.

The foot's movable parts are the "toes." One toe is much thicker than the others, but this "big toe" is not opposable the way the thumb is. Thus, the foot is not usually used to control tools. However, some people who lack or cannot use their hands have learned to use their feet in a variety of activities, such as painting and writing.

Write it: In an essay, compare and contrast a car and a bus.

Hints:
• Before writing, list at least three ways a car and a bus are similar and three ways they are different. If you can list more, do so. You can later choose which similarities and differences to include when writing your paper.
• Decide on your focus. Will you stress the similarities or the differences?
• Give your paper a descriptive title. It might reveal whether you are focusing on the similarities or the differences.

Prompts for Comparing Things Made by People

Write an essay that compares and contrasts a triangle and a square.

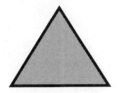

Write an essay that compares and contrasts a clock and a thermometer.

Write an essay that compares and contrasts a telescope and a microscope.

Write an essay that compares and contrasts a newspaper and a magazine.

Write an essay that compares and contrasts a skateboard and a bicycle.

Write an essay that compares and contrasts a pie and a cake.

Prompts for Comparing Things Found in Nature

Write an essay that compares and contrasts a bird and a fly.

Write an essay that compares and contrasts a tree and a bush.

Write an essay that compares and contrasts an elephant and a whale.

Write an essay that compares and contrasts an apple and an orange.

Write an essay that compares and contrasts a skunk and a porcupine.

Write an essay that compares and contrasts an ant and a termite.

Prompts for Comparing Activities and Actions

Write an essay that compares and contrasts soccer and basketball.

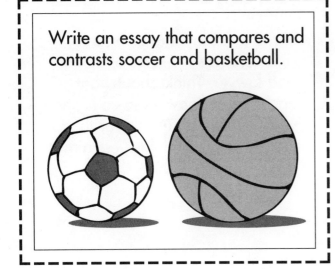

Write an essay that compares and contrasts reading a novel and watching a play.

Write an essay that compares and contrasts laughing and crying.

Write an essay that compares and contrasts hearing and seeing.

Write an essay that compares and contrasts watching TV and listening to the radio.

Write an essay that compares and contrasts winning and losing.

Prompts for Comparing People

Write an essay that compares and contrasts two of your friends. Think about the ways you interact with each of them. Are there some activities you prefer to do with one, and different activities to do with the other?

Write an essay that compares and contrasts the roles of doctor and lawyer. Think about what each has to know. Also consider what doctors aim to do for their patients, and what lawyers aim to do for their clients.

Write an essay that compares and contrasts two heroes from literature. These can be characters from myths, novels, movies, TV shows, or any other kind of story.

Write an essay that compares and contrasts being a student and being a teacher. Think about what it takes to be a good teacher and what it takes to be a good student. Also consider how teachers affect students and how students affect teachers.

Write an essay that compares and contrasts being an infant and being an adult. Think about the activities in a young child's life, and the activities in an adult's life.

Write an essay that compares and contrasts being a musician and being an actor. Think about the tools and materials used by musicians and by actors. Also, think about the ways each affects the audience.

Prompts for Comparing Words and Ideas

Write an essay that compares and contrasts laws and rules. Think about where laws and rules come from, and how they work.

Write an essay that compares and contrasts the concepts *lake* and *ocean*. How can you tell that one body of water is a lake while another is an ocean?

Write an essay that compares and contrasts the meanings of the words *game* and *sport*. What games are sports and what games aren't sports? Are there any sports that are not games?

Write an essay that compares and contrasts *animals* and *plants*. Think about how you know that something is an animal when you see it, and how you know something is a plant when you see it.

Write an essay that compares and contrasts the meanings of the words *city* and *country*. Think about what makes a place a city and what makes a place a country.

Write an essay that compares and contrasts the meanings of the words *want* and *need*. Is it possible to want something and not need it, or need something and not want it?

Comparing: Analogies

Writers often compare subjects that are obviously similar. An example would be comparing dogs and wolves. Sometimes, however, writers compare two subjects that at first seem very different, but that turn out to be alike in many ways. This is called "making an analogy." Analogies are used in many kinds of writing, including poetry and science reports.

Model

Your Mental Diet

Books are like food. Some books, like vegetables, are good for you. For example, a book can enrich your life by teaching you a skill or introducing you to new ideas. Other books may be fun to read but, like candy, in the long run don't contribute to your well-being. Some books might even be bad for you, for example, by wasting your time or by giving you false or misleading information.

Some books are easy to take in, like pudding. Others, like celery, have to be chewed for a while before you can digest them.

You can find books that, like smoked meats, last a long time without going bad. In fact, a few books have stayed "good" for hundreds and even thousands of years. Other books, like bread, get stale quickly. Although popular at first, after a while almost no one reads them.

Which kinds of books should you "eat"? As with real food, that decision is yours. But it is one you should take seriously.

Write it: Write an essay that develops the following analogy: "A school is like a factory."

Hints:
• Before writing, ask yourself a few questions: What is the goal of a factory and what is the goal of a school? What do you need to have a factory and what do you need to have a school? How are all factories alike and how are all schools alike?
• Give your paper a descriptive title.
• In the first paragraph, introduce the comparison.

More Analogy Prompts

Explain how the human brain is like a library. Or, if you can think of something else that is like the human brain, use that comparison to build an analogy.

Explain how a family is like a sports team. Or, if you can think of something else that is like a family, use that comparison to build an analogy.

Explain how writing a story is like taking a trip. Or, if you can think of another activity that is like writing a story, use that comparison to build an analogy.

Explain how a law is like a dog's leash. Or, if you can think of something else that is like a law, use that comparison to build an analogy.

Explain how punctuation marks are like a traffic officer. Or, if you can think of something else that is like punctuation marks, use that comparison to build an analogy.

Explain how television is like candy. Or, if you can think of something else that is like television, use that comparison to build an analogy.

Condensing an Article

Busy readers appreciate concise information. For this reason, writers often condense a text. This means leaving out less important details so that readers can focus on what's most important.

Model

Helping a Lightning Victim (original version)

Although lightning can be deadly, most lightning-strike victims survive. More could be saved if bystanders took the proper action. Don't be afraid to touch a victim. The person does not retain a charge. When lightning strikes someone, the electrical force may interrupt the person's breathing. Immediately start "Rescue Breathing." Lay the victim face up, pinch the victim's nose, and clear any blockage from the airway. Now take a deep breath, open your mouth wide, place it over the victim's mouth, and blow air into the victim until the person's chest rises. Remove your mouth from the victim's and watch the person's chest fall as air escapes. Repeat the activity every 5 seconds, 12 breaths per minute, until help arrives. If the person's heart has stopped, try to restart it if you are trained in Cardiopulmonary Resuscitation (CPR).

Helping a Lightning Victim (condensed version)

If someone hit by lightning stops breathing, immediately start "Rescue Breathing." Lay the victim face up, pinch the person's nose, clear airway blockages, take a big breath, place your open mouth over the victim's mouth, and blow until the person's chest rises. Remove your mouth and wait for the person's chest to fall. Repeat every 5 seconds until help arrives. If the person's heart has stopped and if you know CPR, use it.

Write it: Condense the text below to half its length or less:
You may know that the earth travels around the sun at about 66,500 miles (107,000 km) per hour. But did you realize that the sun itself is moving around our galaxy, known as the Milky Way? The Milky Way itself moves around a cluster of other galaxies. The cluster itself is moving relative to other galaxies.

Hints:
- Omit facts and words not needed to get across the main idea.
- Try substituting shorter words or phrases.
- Try merging sentences.

More Articles to Condense

Condense the text to half its length or less.

Many people believe that the steam engine was invented three centuries ago. After all, Thomas Savery patented the device in 1698.

However, like many inventions, the steam engine has a very long history. About 2,000 years ago, Hero, a Greek inventor, built the aeolipile: a boiler with a hollow ball hanging above it. The ball had two nozzles. When steam flowed into the ball and escaped from the nozzles, the ball revolved, like a lawn sprinkler.

Condense the text to half its length or less.

The word *equator* may make you think of hot temperatures. But you could visit certain places in the equatorial zone and actually freeze to death.

Why? Several mountains are located on or near the equator. For example, Africa's Mount Kenya, just south of the equator, is about 17,000 feet (5,200 m) high. Near the top, you will find year-round glaciers. Likewise, in Ecuador (named for the equator) Mount Chimborazo is perpetually topped with snow.

Condense the text to half its length or less.

In 1927, Charles Lindbergh became the first person to fly *solo* across the Atlantic. But he was not the first person to make a transatlantic flight. That honor is shared by John Alcock and Arthur Brown, who made the trip eight years before Lindbergh, in June 1919.

Later, British and German dirigibles carried 64 people across the ocean. Thus, Lindbergh was "only" the 67th person to fly across the Atlantic, but the difficulty of doing it alone made his accomplishment historic.

Descriptive Writing

Descriptive writing involves creating word pictures in the reader's mind. Your goal is to get the reader to see what you see. In some cases, descriptive writing also includes sharing other sensory information, for example, sounds and smells.

Model

Dear Jennifer,

I enjoyed your e-mail about the rocket launch you saw at Cape Canaveral. From what you wrote, I could tell it was a lot different from seeing it on TV, especially the part about the ground shaking.

Nothing nearly as exciting has been happening here, but there was something a bit strange. The other evening, I was baby-sitting at a neighbor's place while my parents were at the movies. When I got home, I found the front door swung open. I had read an article about the danger of entering a house if a robber is inside, so I ran to a neighbor's home and called 911. A police car soon arrived and two officers went into my house while I stayed outside.

After a while, one officer came out and motioned me to follow him inside. He said, "I think you did have a break-in." He led me down the hall to my room. I peeked inside and saw drawers open with clothing hanging out, the contents of my backpack emptied all over the floor.

The other officer said, "Someone must have gone through here looking for money or jewelry. Can you tell if anything is missing?"

How embarrassing. The room was exactly as I left it when I had rushed out to my baby-sitting job.

Write it: Create a word picture of the room you are in right now.

Hints:
• Before writing, observe the room carefully. Jot down a few notes of interesting details.
• Think up a word or phrase that sums up your feelings about the room. For example, is it neat or cozy or busy?
• Now describe the room so that someone who isn't there could imagine what it is like. If you like, in addition to visual details, use other sensory information, such as sounds that you hear.

More Descriptive Writing: A Person

Create a word picture of the person shown here.

More Descriptive Writing: A Place

Create a word picture of the place shown here.

More Descriptive Writing: A Thing

Create a word picture of the thing shown here.

Descriptive Writing: Actions

To describe people and things in motion, think of yourself as a video camera. Try to capture sights and sounds. This kind of descriptive writing plays a part in many assignments, including articles, stories, and science reports.

Model
Ryland Talking on the Telephone

The phone rings. My 15-year-old brother Ryland answers it. "Hi, Kyle," he says to the person at the other end of the line. Kyle is my brother's best friend. He is also a great talker. He talks and talks and never stops to listen. This makes it easy for Ryland to continue doing his history homework while listening to Kyle.

Ryland tilts his head slightly to keep the receiver in place while he uses his hands to flip the pages in his textbook and takes notes. My brother looks at me and rolls his eyes upward, as if to say, "I can't believe the stupid things I'm listening to." I'm about to start laughing, but he puts a finger across his mouth, telling me to keep quiet.

Now Kyle must have said something that makes sense because Ryland is nodding. I don't know why he bothers to nod since Kyle isn't in the room and can't see the gesture.

Finally, Ryland looks at the clock. It's nearly 8:30. Ryland's favorite TV program is coming on. Into the phone he says, "I have to go now. I have a lot of homework to do."

Right!

Write it: Describe someone engaged in an everyday activity such as eating a difficult-to-eat food or learning to ride a bicycle.

Hints:
• Before writing, try to see the activity in your mind. Or if it's something you can observe, watch before you write.
• Describe the activity in the present tense, as if it's happening right now.
• Include details so that readers can "see" the action as they read your words.
• Give your description a specific title.

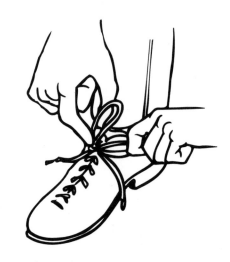

More Actions to Describe

Describe someone preparing something to eat, for example, pizza or a cake. Include details so that the readers can "see" the action as they read.

Describe someone playing a musical instrument, such as a piano or a guitar. Include details so that the readers can "see" the action as they read.

Describe someone playing a game. It could be someone engaged in a sport, for example, dribbling and shooting a basketball. Or it could be a baby playing with a toy. Include details so that the readers can "see" the action as they read.

Describe someone doing a chore, such as washing dishes, mowing the lawn, doing the laundry, or painting a wall. Include details so that the readers can "see" the action as they read.

Describe someone engaged in a pastime, such as sewing, knitting, making a model, reading, or working at a computer. Include details so that the readers can "see" the action as they read.

Describe an animal in motion, for example, a dog scratching fleas, a fly buzzing at a window, or a cat stalking a bird. Include details so that the readers can "see" the action as they read.

More Actions to Describe: Sand Sculpting

Translate the pictures into a description of the activity.

More Actions to Describe: Tying a Bow Tie

Translate the pictures into a description of the activity.

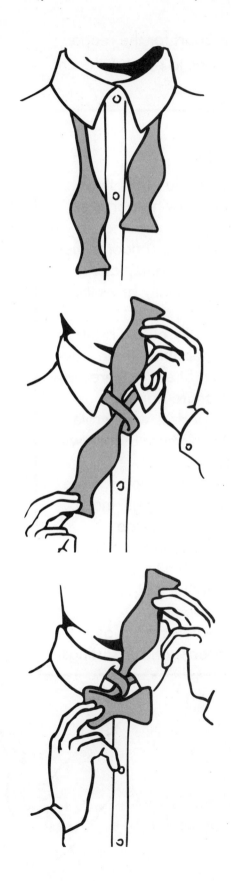

Descriptive Writing: Analysis

One way to describe a complex object is to take it apart for the reader. This is called *analytical writing*. It involves using words to point out each important piece of the thing.

Model

Analyzing the Front Page

A newspaper's front page is more complex than you might think. Most papers' front pages have some or all of the following parts:

The **nameplate**, which appears centered at the top, gives the paper's name, for example, *The Chicago Tribune* or *The London Times*. Sometimes the newspaper's slogan appears under the nameplate.

The **folio line** appears under the nameplate and usually gives the date of the issue and the price.

The **lead story** appears below the folio line, usually on the right-hand side of the page. A story's title is called the **headline**. If the lead story is unusually important—"UFO Lands on Main Street"—there might be a **banner headline** that runs across the entire paper.

The **byline** gives the name of the reporter or reporters who wrote the story. If the story is about someplace out of town, there usually will be a **dateline** that names the story's location and date.

The text of each story fits into **columns**. In some newspapers, there are up to eight columns. **Art** refers to photographs, drawings, maps, and diagrams. Often a short text called a **caption** will provide information about the art, for example, naming individuals shown.

If an article is long, a **subhead** might be used as a title for a section of the story. When a story continues on another page, a **jump line** directs readers to the appropriate page and column.

The **index** tells readers where to find regular features, such as classified ads, business news, editorials, letters, sports, and TV listings.

Write it: Describe your hand analytically. Name the parts, describe them, and explain their uses.

Hints:
• Start with a descriptive title.
• Write a short introduction that explains what a hand is.
• Don't skip around. Look for a logical way to organize the description.

More Analytical Prompts

Describe a computer analytically. Start by giving an overview, and then discuss each important part.

Describe a ballpoint pen analytically. Start by giving an overview and then discuss each important part.

Describe a pair of eyeglasses analytically. Start by giving an overview and then discuss each important part.

Describe a shirt analytically. Start by giving an overview and then discuss each important part.

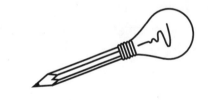

Describe a face analytically. Start by giving an overview and then discuss each important part.

Describe a telephone analytically. Start by giving an overview and then discuss each important part.

Descriptive Writing: Groups

A group is a collection of related things. For example, the group known as "footwear" includes shoes, boots, slippers, sandals, moccasins, and even skates. When writing about a group, you need to show the small differences between the related members.

Model

Seven Different Days

Everyone knows that a week consists of seven days, and that every day of the week consists of twenty-four hours. From the point of view of a clock, Monday is the same as Tuesday or Thursday. But from a human point of view, each day of the week is unique.

Monday is get-going day. Monday may make you feel nervous. There's so much to do and you have to begin to do it.

Tuesday is a high-energy day. No turning back now. You're up to speed.

Wednesday is balancing day. Looking back, you can see what you've accomplished so far. Often, it's more than you expected. You can also look ahead and see that the end of the week is in sight.

Thursday is the high-speed day. You have momentum now.

Friday is relief day. As soon as you finish it, you can relax.

Saturday is play day. You can sleep late unless someone has given you a chore or you have given yourself a task.

Sunday starts out calm. But sometimes it turns into worry day if you didn't finish your work from the old week or if you think too much about the coming week. However, remember, by the end of Sunday, there are only five full days until Saturday. Just 120 hours.

Write it: Write an essay that describes the members of the group called "hobbies." Describe at least three members of this group.

Hints:
• Before writing, brainstorm a list of hobbies.
• Choose the hobbies that you know something about.
• Think about what makes each hobby special. Consider what it involves and what kind of person is likely to have it.
• Give your essay a descriptive title.

More Prompts for Describing Groups

Describe at least three members of the group labeled **books**. Think about the different kinds of books you have seen. Also, think about the people who read the different kinds of books.

Describe at least three members of the group labeled **gifts**. Think about the different kinds of gifts you have given and received, such as "perfect gifts" and "silly gifts" and "bad gifts."

Describe at least three members of the group labeled **motor vehicles**. Think about the different kinds of vehicles and how they are used. Also think about the kinds of people who drive these vehicles.

Describe at least three members of the group labeled **movies**. Think about the kinds of movies you like and the movies you don't like. Also, think about movies that your friends and relatives like or dislike.

Describe at least three members of the group labeled **clothing**. Think about the different kinds of clothing and how each is used. Also think about the kinds of people who wear the clothing.

Describe at least three members of the group labeled **school subjects**. Think about the subjects that you like and those that you don't. Also, think about the value of each subject.

Descriptive Writing: Sounds

You can tell your readers about sounds in three ways. First, you can name something that makes a sound, for example, "A man was talking" or "I heard a car engine start."

Second, you can describe a sound by using a word that imitates it, for example: "The owl *screeched* and the mosquito *buzzed*." Using words that imitate sounds is called onomatopoeia.

Third, you can make a comparison: "The officer's voice was like thunder."

Often, a writer uses two or three of these methods to capture the sounds of a place.

Model

The Clothes Dryer's Music

I'm trying to read a book, but at the moment I can't concentrate. I'm distracted by the sound of our clothes dryer, which is located in the hallway.

Actually, the dryer doesn't make one single sound. It's more like a symphony. First, there is the motor sound. The motor hums constantly. Next, there is a ka-thunk, ka-thunk sound of clothing tumbling. It's a low sound that reminds me of the beat of a bass drum.

Finally, there's a higher-pitched clinking, maybe made by metal buttons on a shirt.

I don't mind the sounds. They're comforting in a way, reminding me that in a few hours I'll have clean clothes to wear.

Write it: Write an essay about the sounds of a room in your house. Use at least two of the three methods for describing sounds: naming what makes the sound, imitating the sound (onomatopoeia), and comparing the sound to another sound.

Hints:
• Before writing, choose a certain time of the day that you will be writing about, for example, morning or dinner.
• Think about all the things in the place that make sounds.
• Give your essay a descriptive title.

More Sound Prompts

Write a sound essay about the radio. Use at least two of the three methods for describing the sounds. You could concentrate on the sounds from a single station, or you could describe the sounds heard as you turn the dial and listen to several stations.

Write a sound essay about neighborhood sounds. These are sounds heard outside your home. Use at least two of the three methods for describing the sounds. Think about the people and objects that make sounds.

Write a sound essay about sounds coming from your TV. Use at least two of the three methods for describing the sounds. Choose a program or a commercial, then turn your back to the set and listen to the sounds.

Write a sound essay about a place where food is served, for example, your school cafeteria. Use at least two of the three methods for describing the sounds. Think about the people and objects that make sounds. Think about the sounds of food being served and eaten.

Write a sound essay about the school playground or a local park. Use at least two of the three methods for describing the sounds. Think about the sounds made by people and also the sounds made by objects, such as the swings.

Write a sound essay about the sounds heard at a sporting event, such as a basketball game, a baseball game, or soccer game. Use at least two of the three methods for describing the sounds. Think about the sounds coming from the players and also from the spectators.

Descriptive Writing: Zooming In

A TV camera can zoom in on a subject until the lens focuses on a single detail. Using your imagination, you can use words in the same way to give readers a close-up picture of a person, place, or thing. This kind of zoom-in description can add interest and excitement to your writing.

Model

Zooming In on Mr. X

Mr. X lives in our apartment building. He is an ordinary looking man. You would probably not notice him if you passed him on the street. But if you saw him as often I do, you'd get the feeling that there's something unusual about him. Then you might notice his lips. They're always moving.

When I first noticed this, I thought he was about to say something to me. But he said nothing. Although I wanted to know what was going on, I didn't know how to ask in a polite way.

Then one day, while I was sitting on the front stoop, I saw him walking up the street, his lips moving as usual. I was so focused on them that when he looked up and saw me, I froze and wasn't able to look away.

He approached and asked, "Why were you staring?" I hesitated, ready to deny it, but his expression convinced me that he wasn't angry. I told him that I noticed his lips were moving. He smiled as if hearing this for the first time. Then he said, "You know how some people move their lips when they read? I guess my lips move when I think. I used to talk aloud to myself, but that bothered people so I now do it silently."

Naturally, I wanted to know what he was thinking about. But I didn't know how to ask.

Write it: Think about someone you know very well. Write a zoom-in description that focuses on one important detail about that person's appearance or behavior.

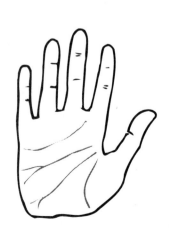

Hints:
• Before you write, list several people that you know. For each, give an unusual detail. It might be one person's unusual hairstyle, and another person's habit of chewing gum.
• To build interest, you might begin your description at a distance, and then come in close on the detail.

More Zoom-In Prompts

Write a zoom-in description of a manufactured object. It could be something common, like a coin, a pencil, or a telephone. Or it could be something that is one-of-a-kind, for example, a ring. Give an overall picture of the object, and then focus on a detail.

Write a zoom-in description of a building. It could be your school, your home, or some other building that you are familiar with. Start with a word picture of the entire front of the building, then move in for a detail.

Write a zoom-in description of something that relates to a plant. It could be a leaf, a root, or a piece of fruit. You might want to use a magnifying glass to study the object before you write. Describe the overall thing, and then focus on a detail.

Write a zoom-in description of a photograph. It could be from a magazine, a newspaper, or your own collection. Describe the overall picture, and then focus on a detail.

Write a zoom-in description of an animal. It could be a pet, for example, a dog or cat. Or it could be an insect or a bird. Give an overall picture of the animal, and then focus on a detail.

Write a zoom-in description of a face. It could be the face of a friend or classmate or relative. Or it could be your own face seen in a mirror. Give an overall picture of the face, and then focus on a detail.

Elaborating Fiction

Writers often start with a short version of a story and expand it. To do so, they add details, actions, and dialogue.

Model

Short Version of The Snake and the Porcupine

One winter day, a porcupine came to a snake's cave and asked to come in. The snake said yes. But when the porcupine was inside, his quills stuck the snake. The snake asked the porcupine to leave. "Not me," said the porcupine. "If you don't like it here, you go."

Expanded Version of The Snake and the Porcupine

One winter day, a shivering porcupine came to a cave. Peering inside, he saw that this was the home of a snake, who was coiled around a fire.

"Can I come in?" pleaded the porcupine, his voice trembling.

The snake said, "This is a small cave."

"No problem," said the porcupine. "I'm skinny."

"OK," said the snake, "I'll try to make room for you."

The porcupine entered and moved near the fire. Unfortunately, his quills kept sticking the snake. Finally, the snake said, "This isn't working. I'll have to ask you to leave."

"Are you kidding?" said the porcupine. "I'm happy here. If you don't like it, you leave."

Write it: Rewrite the following story so that it is at least twice as long. Add details and dialogue.

The Goose That Laid Golden Eggs

A husband and wife owned a goose that laid a golden egg every day. Though other people thought they were lucky, the couple wanted even more gold. They thought they could find it by cutting open the goose, which they did. But there was no gold in there and the goose was dead.

Hints:

• Try to see the action in your mind. Describe details not found in the original version.

• Imagine what the characters might say to each other and include their dialogue. When writing dialogue, start a new paragraph and put the words inside quotation marks.

More Prompts for Elaborating Fiction

Rewrite this fable. Add details so that it is at least twice as long.

The Fox and the Grapes

A fox came upon a grapevine. The grapes grew near the top of the vine. After realizing that the fruit was out of reach, the fox said, "Those grapes are probably sour. I wouldn't eat them even if I could reach them."

Rewrite this fable. Add details so that it is at least twice as long.

The Hare and the Hound

A hound was chasing a hare. But after a while, the hare escaped. A goatherd watched and said "The little hare runs faster than you." "True," said the hound, "but I was running only for food. The hare was running for his life."

Rewrite this fable. Add details so that it is at least twice as long.

The Ant and the Grasshopper

All summer, the grasshopper played while the ant tended its garden. When winter came, the grasshopper was hungry and begged the ant for food. But the ant said, "You were silly to spend your summer not working."

Rewrite this fable. Add details so that it is at least twice as long.

Belling the Cat

The mice were tired of the cat sneaking up on them. One mouse said "Let's tie a bell to the cat's neck. It'll warn us."

The mice thought that this was a fine idea until a wise mouse said, "Who will tie the bell to the cat's neck?"

Rewrite this fable. Add details so that it is at least twice as long.

The Milkmaid's Chickens

A milkmaid who had just milked her cow said, "I'll make butter, trade the butter for eggs, raise chickens, get more eggs until I'm rich."

But she didn't watch her step. She tripped, spilled the milk, and ended up with no chickens.

Rewrite this fable. Add details so that it is at least twice as long.

The Boy and the Almonds

A little boy reached into a jar of almonds and filled his hand. But then he couldn't get the fist full of nuts out. Finally, he began to cry.

A friend said, "If you drop half the nuts, your fist will be small enough to get out of the jar."

Elaborating Nonfiction

One way to write an article is to start with a short version and expand it. This involves adding details and interesting information.

Model

Short Version of "How to Catch a Baseball Barehanded"

1. Put out your hand.
2. When the ball makes contact with your hand, grab it.

Expanded Version of "How to Catch a Baseball Barehanded"

A baseball glove makes catching a ball easy and comfortable, especially if the ball is coming fast. However, you don't need a glove to catch a ball. In the early days of the game, no players wore gloves. They caught the balls barehanded. So can you. Here's how:

1. When a ball comes toward you, watch it. Although you can catch a ball without looking at it, you'll have more success by keeping your eye on the ball. You can practice this skill by having someone gently toss the ball in your direction while you watch its flight.

2. As the ball approaches, put both hands between you and the ball. This way, you can guide your hands to the right location and do what experienced players do: "Look the ball into your hands."

3. When the ball makes contact, immediately relax your hands, allowing the ball to push them. If you keep your hands rigid, the ball will likely bounce away as if hitting a wall.

4. Grasp the ball with both hands. Although you can catch a ball one-handed, you're more likely to hold onto it if you use both hands.

Write it: Rewrite the following set of directions so that it is at least twice as long. Add an introduction that gives advice and interesting information.

Sharpening a Pencil Using a Hand-cranked Sharpener
1. Put the pencil in the sharpener.
2. Turn the handle.

Hints:
• Brainstorm details not found in the original version.
• Imagine questions that a reader might ask, and give the answers.
• Add an introduction that explains why someone might try the activity.
• Add steps if needed and add details to steps already given.

More Prompts for Elaborating Nonfiction

Expand these directions to make them complete. Start with a short introduction. You can add steps. The new piece should be at least twice as long as the original.
Brushing Your Teeth
1. Put toothpaste on the brush.
2. Brush the teeth.
3. Rinse your mouth.
4. Put the brush away.

Expand these directions to make them complete. Start with a short introduction. You can add steps. The new piece should be at least twice as long as the original.
Making a Bed
1. Smooth the sheets.
2. Pull the sheets toward the head of the bed.
3. Pull the bedspread up.

Expand these directions to make them complete. Start with a short introduction. You can add steps. The new piece should be at least twice as long as the original.
Making a Phone Call
1. Punch in the number.
2. Talk.
3. Say "Goodbye."
4. Hang up.

Expand these directions to make them complete. Start with a short introduction. You can add steps. The new piece should be at least twice as long as the original.
Threading a Needle
1. Hold the needle in one hand.
2. Hold the thread in the other.
3. Push the end of the thread through the eye of the needle.

Expand these directions to make them complete. Start with a short introduction. You can add steps. The new piece should be at least twice as long as the original.
Using a Dictionary
1. Open the dictionary.
2. Turn to the right page.
3. Read the information.
4. Close the book.

Expand these directions to make them complete. Start with a short introduction. You can add steps. The new piece should be at least twice as long as the original.
Giving a Speech
1. Move to the speaking area.
2. Deliver your speech.
3. Leave the speaking area.

Explaining Behavior

Human behavior can be puzzling. For example, each winter, a group of people known as the "Polar Bears" go for an icy swim.

Writers not only describe such strange behavior, but also try to explain it. This involves figuring out the motives or reasons for the action.

Model

Why Do People Go to Scary Movies?

Although not everyone likes scary movies, millions of people do. Terrifying films like *Alien* and *Jaws* were big hits around the world. This at first may seem odd, because most people avoid scary situations in their actual lives. But there are three reasons why people pay money for the privilege of screaming.

First, scary films are more exciting than ordinary life. If you're like most people, you get up, have the same old breakfast, go to school or work, and see the same friends. There are no big surprises. It can be boring. That's very different from what happens in a movie like *Jaws*, where you never know when a big shark is going to start chasing you.

Second, and more important, scary films give you a chance to test your courage. Although ordinary life often presents difficult problems, those problems are usually not as frightening as doing battle with a slimy monster from another planet or with a huge, hungry shark. Although you don't actually have to do anything while watching a scary movie, you can imagine what you might do.

Third, you get to see that the problems of everyday life are not as bad as they might be. After all, on your worst day, you're not likely to be chased by a monster that is determined to devour you.

Write it: Write an essay that explains why people watch TV. Give at least two reasons.

Hints:
• Before you write, brainstorm as many reasons for watching TV as you can. Then, pick out the most important two or three reasons.
• When you write, begin with a paragraph that briefly describes the behavior and why it is puzzling.

More Behavior Prompts

Write an essay that explains why people give each other presents. Include at least two reasons for the behavior.

Write an essay that explains why people have hobbies, such as stamp collecting or making models. Include at least two reasons for the behavior.

Write an essay that explains why people go to the movies. Include at least two reasons for the behavior.

Write an essay that explains why people smile when they greet each other. Include at least two reasons for the behavior.

Write an essay that explains why people read books. Include at least two reasons for the behavior.

Write an essay that explains why people play sports, such as soccer or basketball. Include at least two reasons for the behavior.

Explaining with Diagrams

A diagram is an outline that gives information by labeling an object's parts. An introduction may give information about the object's history and use. Diagrams are used in science, geography, engineering, sports, manufacturing, archeology, and other fields.

Model

Diagram of a Liquid Fuel Rocket

About a thousand years ago, Chinese scientists invented the solid fuel rocket. In the early twentieth century, American Robert Goddard developed a more controllable liquid fuel rocket, making possible space exploration. Although complex, rockets consist of only six key elements.

1. Shell or skin: This is made of lightweight metal to maximize the payload (astronauts, materials) that can be fired into space.

2. Tank for liquid fuel: The liquid fuel is usually kerosene, which is manufactured from petroleum. In the nineteenth century, kerosene was burned in lamps. Today, it is also used for heating and as a fuel for jet engines.

3. Tank for liquid oxygen: Oxygen is required to burn the fuel. Although it is a gas under everyday conditions, supercooled oxygen is a liquid.

4. Pump: This device moves the fuel and oxygen into the combustion chamber.

5. Combustion chamber: The burning fuel releases fast-moving gases.

6. Exhaust port: As predicted by Newton's Third Law, the rocket moves in the opposite direction of the gases escaping through this opening.

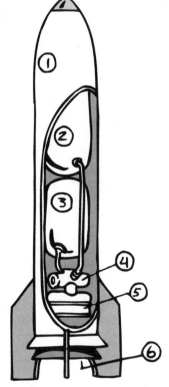

Write it: Draw a simple picture of a telephone. Label the important parts, explaining what each does.

Hints:
- If you can't think of the exact name of a part, use a descriptive word.
- Before you write the labels, think about how you use the phone.
- Add an introduction that would explain what the device is to someone who never saw it before.

More Diagram Prompts

Draw a simple outline picture of a belt and tell what each part does. Add an introduction that explains what a belt is to someone who never saw one.

Draw a simple outline picture of a watch and tell what each part does. Add an introduction that explains what a watch is to someone who never saw one.

Draw a simple outline picture of a bicycle and tell what each part does. Add an introduction that explains what a bicycle is to someone who never saw one.

Draw a simple outline picture of a pencil and tell what each part does. Add an introduction that explains what a pencil is to someone who never saw one.

Draw a simple outline picture of a camera and tell what each part does. Add an introduction that explains what a camera is to someone who never saw one.

Draw a simple outline picture of a shoe and tell what each part does. Add an introduction that explains what a shoe is to someone who never saw one.

Explaining with Examples

If you want people to understand what you're writing, follow up your big ideas with specific examples. Well-chosen examples not only add clarity to writing, but also add interest.

> ## Model
> ### Being Rich Isn't Always Wonderful
>
> Being rich has many advantages. But sometimes it's not such a good thing. *For example*, if you're rich and people find out about it, they'll often bombard you with requests to contribute to their causes. Also, some people may pretend to be your friend just because they hope to benefit from your wealth. Finally, thieves may decide to target your home because they expect you to keep valuables there.

Write it: Complete the following general statement by providing at least two examples:

We often like things that are big: big buildings, big trees, big airplanes. But bigger isn't always better. For example, . . .

Hints:
• Before you write, brainstorm as many examples as you can. Then pick the best example or examples from your list.
• If you are using more than one example, use transition phrases to let your readers know what is happening. For example, you could write: *Another example is...* or *Let me give you a second illustration...*

More Example Prompts

Complete the following statement by adding one or more examples. Many animals, including insects, sometimes act as if they had human intelligence and emotions. For example...

Complete the following statement by adding one or more examples. Although many people do so, it makes no sense to complain about things that cannot be avoided or changed. For example...

Complete the following statement by adding one or more examples. Movies or books that tell fictional stories can teach valuable lessons about real life. For example...

Complete the following statement by adding one or more examples. Many people wish they could read minds. But if ESP were possible, life would change in unexpected ways. For example...

Complete the following statement by adding one or more examples. Some customs and manners that seem natural to us would puzzle people who come from a different background. For example...

Complete the following statement by adding one or more examples. Some important words in the English language are not big words. In fact, many have five or fewer letters. For example...

Complete the following statement by adding one or more examples. Many things that we take for granted would seem amazing if we stopped and thought about them. For example...

Complete the following statement by adding one or more examples. Sometimes an event that seems unhappy or embarrassing when it happens turns out to have value later on. For example...

Humor: Using Exaggeration

Writers are often advised to tell the truth. Even storytellers usually try to make their stories believable. But to make people laugh, writers know that it pays to stretch the truth a little...or a lot. This kind of humor, which is often found in advertising and stand-up comedy, has a traditional form: the "tall tale."

Model
The Day Dad's Snoring Saved Our Town

We call my dad The Snorer. One time he snored so loud he woke himself. Thinking it was a tornado, he shouted, "Everyone into the cellar!"

Dad snores so loud it bothers the neighbors. One of them is a lawyer, and he got everyone on the block to sign a petition demanding that Dad stop snoring. That was like asking thunder to stop thundering.

Our neighbors were peeved until the day a real tornado happened. It had winds more than 150 miles per hour (240 kilometers per hour). No one heard the storm, of course, because Dad's snoring drowned it out. (We learned what happened later from a pilot who was flying over our town.)

We all would have been blown away except that when the tornado heard Dad's snoring, it must have thought a larger tornado was heading its way, and it fled. You may not believe that tornados are cowards. All I can tell you is that we're still here. If you have a better explanation of what happened, I'm willing to listen to the facts.

Write it: Choose a habit, such as being late or messy or lazy. The habit could belong to you or someone you know. Exaggerate the habit into a tall tale.

Hints:
• Remember that the purpose of a tall tale is humor, not to make fun of someone. Often, tall tale tellers make up a character from scratch.
• Before writing, brainstorm a list of things that might happen because of the habit. Let your imagination soar. The more outrageous the ideas, the better.
• As you write, tell the story as if it had actually happened. A serious tone makes the exaggerations funnier.

More Exaggerations Prompts

Write a humorous story that exaggerates a skill that you or someone else has. It could be a useful skill, such as flipping pancakes, or a more unusual skill, for example, being able to talk quickly.

Write a humorous story that exaggerates something unusual that happened during an event, such as a vacation trip or a surprise party.

Write a humorous story that exaggerates an animal's behavior. For example, maybe you have noticed a squirrel busily hiding nuts in your yard. Or perhaps a neighbor's dog constantly barks.

Write a humorous story that exaggerates something about a place. It could be a supermarket or a dentist's office or the home of a friend or relative.

Write a humorous story that exaggerates an unusual object. For example, maybe you have a noisy washing machine or a furnace that makes the house too warm.

Write a humorous story that exaggerates what happened when you tried to learn something. Examples include: learning to ski, learning a part in a play, learning to cook, or learning a school subject.

Humor: Using Puns

A pun is a joke based on homonyms. Homonyms are words that sound alike but have different meanings. An example is *bare* meaning uncovered (a bare head) and *bear* naming a hairy animal (a grizzly bear).

The humor of a pun comes from the fact that the two sound-alike words are deliberately confused, usually in the punch line—the final sentence.

Model

Shoeless and Clueless

The store manager went up to a customer who was wearing no socks and no shoes.

"You'll have to leave immediately," said the manager impatiently. "Can't you read?" The manager pointed to a sign with the words "Bare feet not allowed."

"That doesn't apply to me," answered the customer. "I'm not a bear."

Write it: Make up a punning joke in the form of a very short story. Use one of the following homonym pairs: *beat/beet* or *hole/whole*.

Hints:
• Make sure you understand the meaning of each word. If you don't understand the meaning, check a dictionary. You may discover that some words have many meanings, and this may give you more ideas for your pun.
• Make up several sentences using each word correctly.
• Now, put the wrong homonym into the sentences and see if something funny happens.
• Look for a punch line. In the model above, the punch line is "I am not a bear."
• Write the joke so that it ends with the punch line containing the homonym. Your joke might include the following elements: a setting, characters, actions, and dialogue.
• If you like, give your joke a title.

More Punning Prompts

Make up a punning joke in the form of a very short story. Use one of these homonym pairs:
- *brake/break*
- *cell/sell*
- *dear/deer*

Make up a punning joke in the form of a very short story. Use one of these homonym pairs:
- *hoarse/horse*
- *root/route*
- *sail/sale*

Make up a punning joke in the form of a very short story. Use one of these homonym pairs:
- *die/dye*
- *flea/flee*
- *flour/flower*

Make up a punning joke in the form of a very short story. Use one of these homonym pairs:
- *sent/scent*
- *stake/steak*
- *suite/sweet*

Make up a punning joke in the form of a very short story. Use one of these homonym pairs:
- *foul/fowl*
- *genes/jeans*
- *hair/hare*

Make up a punning joke in the form of a very short story. Use one of these homonym pairs:
- *tail/tale*
- *waist/waste*
- *wait/weight*

Interpreting Proverbs

Interpreting a piece of writing means explaining its meaning. You may need to interpret a text if its meaning is complicated or hard to figure out. For example, proverbs are tricky to understand because they include two messages. One message, called the "specific" or "literal" meaning, is obvious. The second message, called the "general" or "metaphoric" meaning, is hidden. You need to think carefully to uncover it.

Model
Interpreting "Don't cry over spilled milk."

This proverb has the obvious meaning that you shouldn't complain if you or someone else accidentally knock over a glass of milk. Instead of wasting your time complaining, you should try to correct the problem. You could wipe up the spill and pour another glass of milk.

But the proverb has another meaning. You should not complain about <u>any</u> accident. You can't turn back the clock. Instead, you should deal with the results of the event, whatever it is. For example, if you fall and rip your pants, you won't get anywhere by screaming about how new they were or how much they cost. You need to sew or patch the rip, or find someone who knows how to make the repairs. If the pants can't be fixed, then you need to get rid of them and find a way to get a new pair.

Write it: In a paragraph or a short essay, interpret the proverb "You can't judge a book by its cover."

Hints:
• Before writing, try putting the proverb into your own words.
• Think about the literal or obvious meaning of the proverb. Ask yourself what it means to "judge a book." Also, ask *why* you can't judge a book from its cover.
• Try to imagine other actions that are similar to the action of judging a book by its cover.

More Proverbs to Interpret

Read the following proverb:
"People who live in glass houses shouldn't throw stones."
Now interpret it by explaining its literal and general meanings.
Hint: What might happen to the stone throwers?

Read the following proverb:
"Rome wasn't built in a day."
Now interpret it by explaining its literal and general meanings.
Hint: Why does it matter how long it took to build Rome?

Read the following proverb:
"Too many cooks spoil the broth."
Now interpret it by explaining its literal and general meanings.
Hint: Why does having many cooks cause a problem?

Read the following proverb:
"If you want to make an omelet, you have to break some eggs."
Now interpret it by explaining its literal and general meanings.
Hint: Why would someone not want to break the eggs?

Read the following proverb:
"A chain is only as strong as its weakest link."
Now interpret it by explaining its literal and general meanings.
Hint: Why does what happens to one link make a difference to the chain?

Read the following proverb:
"Don't bite off more than you can chew."
Now interpret it by explaining its literal and general meanings.
Hint: What would happen if you bit off more than you could chew?

Read the following proverb:
"Don't bite the hand that feeds you."
Now interpret it by explaining its literal and general meanings.
Hint: What would happen if you did bite the hand that feeds you?

Read the following proverb:
"No use locking the barn door after the horse has been stolen."
Now interpret it by explaining its literal and general meanings.
Hint: When would it make sense to lock the barn door?

Memory Writing: Objects

When writing stories, letters, reports, and other assignments, you sometimes need to use information in your memory. The more you practice memory writing, the better you'll get at it. To check the accuracy of your memory, describe something without looking at it. Later, observe the actual thing.

Model
Describing Our Microwave Oven from Memory

Our microwave sits on a counter in the kitchen. The device is about three feet (1 meter) wide and about one foot (.3 meter) high. It's made out of white metal. The door, which latches on the right, has a window so that you can see what's cooking inside. (However, people in our family usually stand back from the microwave when it's operating.)

The control panel is at the right side of the front. There are 10 buttons with numbers (0 through 9) for setting the length of cooking, and several function keys for controlling various kinds of cooking and for setting the clock.

The cord is thick and dark, ending in a three-prong plug.

Notes based on observation:
1. The machine is actually just under two feet (.6 meter).
2. I forgot the digital clock which is above the control keys.
3. There are actually 12 control keys, including one that turns the clock into a timer and another that adjusts the sounds made by the oven. We don't use most of these keys, which may be why I didn't notice them.

Write it: In a paragraph or a short essay, describe an object that you use almost every day, for example, your toothbrush or a lamp. Include as many details as possible. Think about the parts and how they fit together, as well as the material and color(s). Later, observe the object directly and write notes about details that you omitted or misremembered.

Hints:
• Before writing, try to visualize the object in your imagination.
• Think about times that you have used it.
• Include information relating to all your senses. For example, if the object has a raised portion, you might mention that.

More Objects to Describe from Memory

Clothing: From memory, describe an article of clothing worn often by you or someone you know. It could be a shirt, hat, coat, pants, or shoes. Think about the material, patterns, colors, and condition.

After writing your description, observe the clothing and write about details that you omitted.

Jewelry: From memory, describe a piece of jewelry worn by you or someone you know. It could be a ring, a pendant, a necklace, an earring, a watch, or a pin. Think about the size, the material, color, the overall design, and the parts.

After writing your description, observe the jewelry and write about details that you omitted.

Building: From memory, describe the front of your home or your school. Think about the material, color, windows, doors, street numbers, and other parts.

After writing your description, observe the building and write about details that you omitted or misremembered.

Money: From memory, describe the front of a coin or a piece of paper money. Think about the overall design and its parts. Include information about color and texture.

After writing your description, observe the object and write about details that you omitted or misremembered.

Furniture: From memory, describe a piece of furniture. It could be a chair, a table, or a bed. Think about the material that the thing is made of and the color. Also consider parts, such as drawers or legs.

After writing your description, observe the piece of furniture and write about details that you omitted.

Vehicle: From memory, describe a means of transportation that you frequently use. It could be a car, a bus, a bicycle, or a skateboard. Think about the parts of the vehicle, its color, any decorations, and its overall condition.

After writing your description, observe the vehicle and write about details that you omitted.

Memory Writing: People

Many kinds of writing require you to describe people. Often, this will be done from memory. The more you practice memory writing, the better you'll get at it.

Model

Supermarket Checkout Clerk

I'm in line at our local market. Ahead of me is a man who must have been trying to buy out the store. His shopping cart is filled to the top. As he unloads his selections, the checkout clerk sighs. His white coat is stained and rumpled. He probably has been at work for hours.

He picks up a can of soup and runs it over the scanner. The device "beeps" and an amount appears on the register screen. The clerk repeats the action with another can of soup, then with a can of corn, then with a can of tomatoes. "Beep, beep, beep," says the machine. The clerk looks more and more like a machine, grabbing items, scanning them, and pushing them to a bagger who is trying to keep up.

The checkout clerk shows no emotion. He focuses entirely on his job. He seems neither happy nor sad. Then, a bottle of peppercorns doesn't cause a beep when the clerk scans it. The clerk tries it twice more. The shopper says, "I think those things cost four dollars." The clerk simply picks up a phone. "Price check. Peppercorns. Small bottle."

The answer comes almost immediately. Then the checker punches in the number—four dollars—and resumes scanning items. He says nothing. The machine does all the talking: "Beep, beep, beep."

Write it: Think of someone you have seen engaged in an activity. The activity could be doing a household chore, for example, vacuuming a rug. It could be playing a game, for example, chess. Or it could be paid work, for example, repairing a water main. In a paragraph or a short essay, describe the person's actions.

Hints:
• Before writing, try to visualize the activity in your imagination.
• Jot down details that help tell the story. Include information that comes from all your senses. For example, if the activity involves making sounds, you might mention that in your description.
• Decide whether to describe the action in the present or past tense.

More People to Describe from Memory

Athlete: Choose a sport, such as baseball, basketball, gymnastics, tennis or swimming. From memory, describe an athlete engaged in that activity, for example, a baseball player at bat. Think about details, for example, how the athlete breathes. Your description might also cover equipment used in the sport.

Laborer: From memory, describe someone doing strenuous physical labor. Examples include: digging a ditch, laying bricks, clearing dishes in a restaurant, splitting firewood, shoveling snow, tilling a garden, shingling a roof, and loading or unloading furniture. Your description might also cover equipment used.

Cook: From memory, describe someone preparing food. Examples include: making and baking bread; making pizza dough, rolling or spinning it, and then adding the toppings; preparing and tossing a salad; and making and baking a pie. Your description might include the ingredients and equipment used.

Musician: From memory, describe someone playing a musical instrument. It could be someone you know, or it could be someone you saw on television or at a concert. In your description, include information about how the musician moves. If there was an audience, you might describe how the musician relates to those listening.

Hobbyist: From memory, describe someone involved in an activity. Examples include: gardening, knitting, painting, quilting, sewing, stamp collecting, making models, operating models, solving a crossword puzzle, surfing the Internet, and whittling. Your description might include the materials and equipment used.

Teacher: From memory, describe someone teaching a lesson. This could take place in a regular classroom, or it could be in another kind of learning setting, for example, a club. Think about details, such as how the teacher gets across information. Your description might include materials and equipment used.

Naming Things

Names don't change things. As Shakespeare wrote, "That which we call a rose by any other name would smell as sweet."

Nevertheless, often much creativity goes into deciding what to call something. Some companies spend thousands of dollars finding names for their new products. This usually involves brainstorming many possible names and then choosing a favorite.

One way to practice the activity is to rename familiar things.

Model
Renaming the Bicycle

The word *bicycle* comes from two ancient expressions: *bi* (meaning "two") and *cyclus* (meaning "circle"). Thus, the name *bicycle* is an accurate description. Here are other possible names for the device:

- balancer
- balancycle
- pedalcycle
- ridercycle
- travelcycle
- pedal-go
- pedalwheeler
- solocycle
- soloped
- pumpalong

My choice is *solocycle*. I like the repetition of the *s* sound. The word gets across the idea that the basic device is for one rider. True, there are cycles built for two riders, but I would call them duo-cycles.

Write it: Write an article in which you present a new name for the computer.

Hints:
- Brainstorm at least five possible names. The more names you come up with, the better. You can invent new words or use old words in a new way.
- Write an introduction that gives some information about the device and its old name.
- End with a paragraph that gives your favorite name and explains why you like it best. Reasons might include clarity, sound, and freshness.

More Renaming Prompts

Find a new name for *book*. Think about what books look like and are used for. Try to find a name that is easy to say.

Find a new name for *pencil*. Think about what pencils look like and are used for. Try to find a name that is easy to say.

Find a new name for *hat*. Think about what hats look like and are used for. Try to find a name that is easy to say.

Find a new name for *shoe*. Think about what shoes look like and are used for. Try to find a name that is easy to say.

Find a new name for *light bulb*. Think about what light bulbs look like and are used for. Try to find a name that is easy to say.

Find a new name for *television*. Think about what televisions look like and are used for. Try to find a name that is easy to say.

Find a new name for *map*. Think about what maps look like and are used for. Try to find a name that is easy to say.

Find a new name for *human being*. Think about what human beings look like and do. Try to find a name that is easy to say.

Paraphrasing

Paraphrasing means restating ideas in your own words. This skill is especially important when writing reports using material from many sources. Expressing facts in a single style makes them easier to grasp.

When paraphrasing, you must not change facts or misrepresent the original source. You may move material and omit facts that are not needed. You may also add facts based on prior knowledge if you are certain that the added information is accurate.

Model
Original version:

The peanut is scientifically not considered a nut. True nuts grow on trees. The peanut is actually a member of the pea family. The peanut plant produces its fruit underground in pods that contain from one to three edible seeds. The seeds are consumed in many food products, the most popular being peanut butter.

Paraphrased version:

The word peanut contains the word nut, but the peanut is not actually a nut. Real nuts, such as walnuts, grow on trees. Peanuts, on the other hand, grow on bushes. The pea in peanuts gives a clue about what kind of plant a peanut is. Peanuts are a type of pea. However, while the seeds of common pea plants grow above ground, peanut seeds grow in pods underground. The pods contain one to three seeds. These can be eaten raw or roasted or crushed into peanut butter.

Write it: Paraphrase the following paragraph.

A weed is not a particular kind of plant or a naturally "bad" plant. Rather, the label "weed" is applied to any plant that grows where it is not wanted. For example, to someone who wants a well-manicured lawn, the dandelion is viewed as a weed.

Hints:
• Before writing, carefully read the paragraph. Reread it if you need to.
• On a piece of paper list a few words that will help you remember the most important facts and ideas. Do not write long phrases.
• Put the original text aside and write from memory. Use your notes if you like.

More Prompts for Paraphrasing

Paraphrase the following paragraph. First read it carefully. Take notes if you like. Then put the original away before you write your own version.

Almost everyone is familiar with plastic. This material, manufactured from coal and other organic substances, is used in products ranging from toys to telephones. Although plastic products are known for being solid, oddly the word plastic originally meant something flexible or easily changed. Plastic got its name because, when heated, the material is soft and easily molded.

Paraphrase the following paragraph. First read it carefully. Take notes if you like. Then put the original away before you write your own version.

You are surrounded by millions and millions of factories, though you may never have paid much attention to them. These factories, working silently, combine carbon dioxide from the air with water from the ground to produce many kinds of food. The manufacturing process, which requires sunlight, is called photosynthesis. The factories may be known to you by their more common name: leaves.

Paraphrase the following paragraph. First read it carefully. Take notes if you like. Then put the original away before you write your own version.

Forest fires can be scary and may destroy valuable trees. At the same time, they play a positive role. Although some forest fires are started by people, the great majority are ignited by lightning. Perhaps more surprising, forest fires actually play a role in nature's cycle. For example, the cones of some trees, such as the bristol pine, open only when subjected to intense heat of the kind found in a forest fire.

Personification

You can create interest in an object by personifying it. This means treating the thing as if it were a person able to observe, think, and talk. An example is a TV commercial featuring a talking automobile.

Model

The Birth of the Slinky

I'm the Slinky, one of the most popular toys of modern times. You may have played with me yourself and been amazed how I somersault down the stairs without getting hurt. But I'll bet you don't know how I came to exist.

I was invented by a scientist, not by a toy maker. It was all because of an accident. Does that surprise you? It shouldn't. Many inventions came to be because of something unexpected.

In the 1940s, Richard James was trying to find a way to protect instruments on ships. Often, the motions of waves damaged compasses and other devices. Mr. James thought that he could use springs to solve the problem. One morning, while experimenting in his lab, the scientist accidentally knocked a spring off the shelf. The spring dropped onto a lower shelf. Instead of stopping there, it flipped forward and landed on a pile of books on a table. But it didn't rest there, either. It went head over heels again onto the floor.

A less curious person might have put the spring back on the shelf. But Mr. James decided to figure out why the spring behaved that way. When he told his wife Betty about it, she realized that her husband had discovered a new toy. After studying words in a dictionary for two days, she found the word Slinky, and that's why we're called by the name.

Write it: Think of an object. It should be something that you are familiar with or that you can learn about through research. Write a story or an essay in which the object tells about itself using the first-person pronoun "I."

Hints:

• You might have the object tell how it came to be and how it works.
• You don't have to start your writing with "I am . . . ." You might try to begin with an observation, for example, a pencil might start, "Some people are nervous about writing stories or drawing pictures."
• Give your personification a descriptive title.

More Personification Prompts

Be an animal: You could be a household pet, for example, a dog, a cat, a fish, or a bird. Or you could be a creature from the wild, for example, a rattlesnake, a gorilla, or a whale. Give your view about the world.

Be a place: You could be a public place, such as a park, a skyscraper, a museum, or a theater. Or you could be a private place, for example, a room in your home. Tell about what goes on in this place from your point of view.

Be a character: The character could be a person, for example, The Great Brain or the Wizard of Oz. Or it could be an animal, such as King Kong or Black Beauty. Talk about your experiences in the story that made you famous.

Be a plant: You could be a flower, a weed, a tree, a mushroom, or any other member of the "flora" branch of life. (The other branch is "fauna" —animals.) As a plant, describe what you see, what you feel, what you eat, or your problems.

Be an emotion: You could be happiness, sadness, fear, hope, loneliness, joy, or any other feeling. Describe yourself by telling what it means for someone to experience you. Also, explain why you are important in people's lives.

Be a school subject: You could be art, geography, history, language, math, music, physical education, science, social studies, or any other subject taught in your school. Describe what you are and explain why you are important.

Be a game: You could be baseball, checkers, soccer, or any other game. Imagine that you meet someone who knows nothing about you. Explain what you are. Or you could describe a conversation between you and another game.

Be a tool: You could be a pencil, a toaster, a computer, a lawn mower, a pair of scissors, a scale, a telescope, eyeglasses, or any other useful object. Describe yourself, including your main parts, and how you feel about the work that you do.

Persuasive Writing

Writers often try to convince readers to do something or to believe something. This is called persuasive writing. It usually involves giving facts, opinions, and examples. Persuasive writing is found in advertisements, editorials, and campaign speeches.

Model
Why You Should Learn to Eat with Chopsticks

Chopsticks comes from a Chinese word *k'wai-tsze*, which means "the quick ones." People who are expert at using chopsticks can quickly manipulate the two sticks while eating Chinese cuisine.

Eating with chopsticks isn't difficult. Most people can master the basics in minutes. But because you can always eat with a fork, you may wonder why you should bother with chopsticks. Here are three reasons.

First, chopsticks are designed for eating Chinese food. Most Chinese dishes consist of vegetables, meat, or fish cut into small pieces meant to be picked up by chopsticks.

Second, if you're not Chinese, eating in a Chinese restaurant takes you out of your ordinary environment. Using chopsticks adds to the experience.

Third, if you live in a culture where eating with a fork is common, people will appreciate your skill in using chopsticks. They will know that you took the time to learn the ways of another culture.

Write it: Choose a skill that you have mastered but that many people cannot do, for example, speak a second language or play a musical instrument. Write an essay that attempts to persuade readers to learn that skill.

Hints:
• Before writing, list as many reasons as you can for learning the skill. Then choose the strongest reasons.
• Before writing, think about how to order the reasons. Sometimes, the most effective way is to end with your strongest or most surprising reason.
• Give your essay a specific title.

More Prompts for Persuasive Writing

Write an essay that tries to persuade readers to read one of your favorite books or to see one of your favorite movies. Include at least three reasons in your essay.

Write an essay that tries to persuade readers that colonizing Mars is a good idea or that it is a bad idea. Include at least three reasons in your essay.

Write an essay that tries to persuade readers to watch more television or to watch less television. Include at least three reasons in your essay.

Write an essay that tries to persuade readers that having a pet is a good idea or that it is a bad idea. Include at least three reasons in your essay.

Write an essay that tries to persuade readers to play a sport or a game that you like, or to avoid a sport or game that you dislike. Include at least three reasons in your essay.

Write an essay that tries to persuade readers that animals should—or should not—have the same rights that people have. Include at least three reasons in your essay.

Point of View: First Person

When a writer uses the pronoun *I* or *we*, the story is said to be told in the first person point of view. This point of view brings the storyteller into the action as if he or she were really there. The first person point of view can be used in fiction or nonfiction.

Model

A Scary Airplane Ride

Over the intercom, the pilot announced, "Flight attendants, prepare for departure." Thirty seconds later, the jumbo jet's engines roared briefly and the plane turned onto the main runway. Out the window I could see San Francisco Bay.

The cabin was hushed. Some people, I'm sure, were nervous, but not me. I love the thrill and power of takeoffs.

The plane was now accelerating down the runway. I could see runway markers coming faster and faster, until they merged in a blur. In a second or two we would be off the ground.

But suddenly a horrible squealing noise penetrated my ears, and I was thrown forward hard against the seat belt, almost hitting my head against the seat ahead of me.

A few seconds later, the plane came to a stop. All was silent. Then the intercom crackled and the pilot, in a slightly angry voice, said, "Sorry about that. Seems like someone in the tower forget to tell an incoming plane that we were taking off.
I'm going to turn this bird around, go back to the end of the runway, and try again."

That's exactly what happened. But when the pilot said, "Here we go," this time I was nervous, too.

Write it: Choose an experience that you had. Then write an essay about it using the first person point of view.

Hints:
• Before writing, brainstorm several memorable experiences. To get ideas, think about hobbies, school, sports, travel, and health.
• Give your essay a descriptive title.
• Look for a clear ending.

More Prompts Using the First Person

Use the first person point of view to describe something that you did, for example, act in a play or undergo an operation.

Use the first person point of view to describe something as if an object were talking. For example, you could have your toothbrush or bicycle describe you.

Use the first person point of view to describe an imaginary event. Write as if you were a character involved in the happening.

Use the first person point of view to retell a story that you read or a movie that you saw. Write as if you were the main character in the story.

Use the first person point of view to describe something as an animal might see it, for example, a household pet, an insect, a shark, or a dinosaur.

Use the first person plural point of view to describe an activity that involved other people and you. The event could be a family trip or a picnic or a sporting event.

Point of View: Second Person

Most stories and reports are written using the first-person pronoun (*I* or *we*) or the third-person pronoun (*he, she, it,* or *they*). But using the second-person pronoun (*you*) can add interest.

In the model below, a sports reporter used the "you" technique to capture an exciting moment in a football game. In the story, the pronoun *you* refers to a football player named Terrell Owens. For most of the game, Owens had done poorly. Then, in the final few seconds, he was given one more chance to catch the ball.

Model

Dramatic Touchdown Delivers Redemption
by Tim Keown, *San Francisco Chronicle*, January 4, 1999

You drop four passes, one in the end zone and one that looked like your team's last best chance. You also fumble it away once, the first time you catch the ball. Bad day at the office doesn't begin to cover it.

And then, just when heroism seemed impossible, you're underneath a swarm in the end zone with the ball in your arms. This time you didn't drop it. This time 66,000 people are screaming in your ears, the solid shriek of pure shock. The game is over. You won. You won the game, and the worst game of your life just became the one they'll remember forever.

So, what do you do? This is what you do: You cry. You run off the field with the ball in one hand, your face contorted into a thousand lines of disbelief, the tears coming without embarrassment.

Write it: Choose a person you know who did something interesting, for example, won a contest, built a house, caught a big fish, or rode a giant roller coaster. The person could be a friend or a relative. Describe the event using "you" as if you were telling the story to the person who was involved in it.

Hints:
• Before writing, try to replay the action in your imagination. Make notes about important details.
• Decide what tense to use. "You" stories are usually written in the present tense. This makes the action seem as if it is happening now.
• Give your story a specific title.

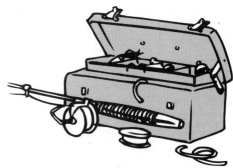

More Prompts Using the Second Person

Write a "you" story or article **about yourself.** Pick an event that you were involved in, such as acting in a play, visiting a landmark, having an operation, or meeting someone famous. Write as if you were talking to yourself. Instead of using the pronoun *I*, use *you*.

Write a "you" story or article **about a place that you know well.** It could be your home or a room in your home, or it could be a public place, such as a park or your school. Write as if you were talking to the place. Explain what makes the place special.

Write a "you" story or article **about a familiar object.** It could be a tool, for example, a computer. Or a model that you built. Or a piece of furniture in your home. Write as if you were talking to the object. Your piece might explain what the object does.

Write a "you" story about a **book.** It could be fiction or nonfiction. Write as if you were talking to the book. Your piece might describe what the book is about and give information about its author. You could also explain why the book is worth reading.

Write a "you" story or article **about a historical figure.** It could be a leader, an explorer, a scientist, an artist, an athlete, a writer, or anyone you know about. Write as if you were talking to the person. You might explain why the person has been remembered over the years.

Write a "you" story or article **about an animal.** It could be a pet, a wild animal, or a fictional creature, such as Jaws. Write as if you were talking to the animal. For example, an article about a boa constrictor might begin: *You squeeze your prey until it cannot breathe.*

Point of View: Third Person

When you write about a subject using pronouns such as *he, she, it,* or *they,* this is called writing in the third person point of view. This approach allows you to stand outside the action. The third person point of view can be used in fiction or nonfiction.

Model

Brothers, Teammates

From the time Orville and Wilbur Wright were little children, they played together, worked together, and thought together. They usually owned all their toys in common and shared their thoughts and dreams. This was how they came to pursue the goal of building a power-driven airplane.

According to a statement that Wilbur published, nearly everything that was done in their lives was the result of conversations, suggestions, and discussions between them.

Write it: Write a third person article about two people you know who work or play together. In the essay, name the people and use third person pronouns such as *he, him, his, she, her, hers, they, them, their,* and *theirs.*

Hints:
• Before you write, list a few twosomes that you know about. They can be people in your life, or people you know through reading or watching TV or movies. These could be neighbors, business partners, or any other two people who are important to each other. Then choose a pair that strongly interests you.
• Think about what makes the two people into a team or couple.
• Give your essay a specific title.

More Prompts Using the Third Person

Use the third person point of view in an essay about an **object**, such as a toy, a tool, or an article of clothing. After introducing the object, refer to it using the third person pronouns *it* and *its*.

Use the third person point of view in an essay about an **event**, such as a flood, a fire, a storm, an earthquake, or a war. After introducing the event, refer to it using third person pronouns, such as *it* or *its*.

Use the third person point of view in an essay about an **animal**. It could be a pet that you own, or it could be a wild animal, such as a squirrel or a mosquito. After introducing the animal, refer to it using third person pronouns, such as *it, its, he, his, him, she, her,* or *hers*.

Use the third person point of view in an essay about a **character** from a book, a movie, a TV show, or a song. Introduce the character and then refer to the character using third person pronouns, such as *he* or *she*.

Use the third person point of view in an essay about a **group** of things, such as the buildings in your neighborhood or the books in your local library. After introducing the group, refer to it using third person pronouns, such as *they, them,* and *their*.

Use the third person point of view to describe **yourself**. You could focus on a skill or on an experience you had. However, instead of referring to yourself as "I," refer to yourself using *he* or *she*, as if you were writing about someone else.

Pros and Cons

Writers sometimes lay out the good points and bad points of a subject. The good points are called the "pros" or benefits. The bad points are called the "cons."

This type of writing is found in articles meant to help readers make a decision, for example, whether or not to buy a product or try a hobby. The challenge is to make the presentation balanced.

Model

Making Them Laugh

Many people fantasize about becoming a stand-up comedian. They want to be the next Bill Cosby, Woody Allen, or Bob Hope.

This dream is not surprising. When you make people laugh, you know they are happy. You also have the stage all to yourself. If you succeed, it's not because of a group. It's your sense of humor, your timing, and your stage presence. It's just you and the audience.

Of course, when you flop as a stand-up comedian—and even the best comedians sometimes flop—there is no one around to share the blame. The room becomes eerily quiet, except for a few people coughing. You begin to sweat. You try harder, but that only makes your routine less funny. Professional comedians call this "dying."

Is it worth being a comedian when you can fail in such a public way? It depends on how much you want to entertain people and how much you fear falling on your face.

Write it: Choose an activity that you know a lot about, for example, building models, going to camp, or learning a musical instrument. Then write about the pros and cons of that activity.

Hints:
• Before writing, brainstorm a list of pros and cons about your activity. Then choose the ones that seem most important.
• Give your article a specific title.
• Start with a sentence or paragraph that introduces the activity.
• Include a real ending. It doesn't have to tell which side you think is stronger, but it should give readers something to think about.

More Pros and Cons Prompts

Write a pros and cons article about having or not having an after-school job, such as baby-sitting or working in a store. Make the article balanced so that a reader could not tell which side you favor.

Write a pros and cons article about being taller than average or being shorter than average. Make the article balanced so that a reader could not tell which side you favor.

Write a pros and cons article about being a super genius. Make the article balanced so that a reader could not tell which side you favor.

Write a pros and cons article about watching television. Make the article balanced so that a reader could not tell which side you favor.

Write a pros and cons article about space exploration. Make the article balanced so that a reader could not tell which side you favor.

Write a pros and cons article about having a pet. Make the article balanced so that a reader could not tell which side you favor.

Questioning

Ideas for writing often grow from questions. The more questions you ask about things, the better. So how can you improve your skill at asking questions? Try writing question lists. Just choose a topic and ask away.

Model

What About Eggs?

Eggs are a common food. Our refrigerator is always filled with plenty of eggs. We eat them for breakfast, and we eat them in baked desserts. I not only have a lot of experience eating eggs, but I also have a lot of questions about them. Here are examples:

Where did the idea of Easter eggs come from?
Are eggs healthy to eat?
Do all people eat eggs?
Does a chick know that it's in an egg?
Do all birds lay eggs?
Do all eggs have the same "egg" shape?
Does anything else in the world have an "egg" shape?
Do all birds lay the same number of eggs in a year?
Do all eggs hatch in the same amount of time?
Why are eggs sold by the dozen? Are they sold that way everywhere?
How long can eggs be stored before they go bad?
How are eggshells used?

Write it: Choose a familiar topic—such as "the wind" or "time" or any sport you play—and write a question list. See if you can think up at least 10 questions.

Hints:
- Give your list a specific title.
- Write a short introduction.
- Include at least some questions whose answers you don't know.

More Questioning Prompts

List at least 10 questions about **airplanes**. Consider airplanes you've flown in, seen, or read about. Begin your piece with a short introduction.

List at least 10 questions about **dreams**. Think about kinds of dreams and the meaning of dreams. Begin your piece with a short introduction.

List at least 10 questions about **clothing**. Think about the history of clothes, and also their design and manufacturing. Begin your piece with a short introduction.

List at least 10 questions about **UFOs** (unidentified flying objects). Think about UFOs featured in movies and novels as well as in news reports. Begin your piece with a short introduction.

List at least 10 questions about **computers**. Think about computers of the past, the present, and the future. Begin your piece with a short introduction.

List at least 10 questions about **paper**. Think about different kinds and uses of paper. Begin your piece with a short introduction.

Ranking

Writers often put items in order of quality, for example, "The Year's Top Ten Songs." This is called "ranking." Usually, the writer includes an introduction to the list, and a comment on each item.

Model
The Five Worst Restaurants in Town

Our town has many fine restaurants. No matter what kind of food you like—Mexican, Italian, Chinese, whatever—you can find it. On the other hand, we also have some bad restaurants. Here are five that you should avoid even if you're starving. The ranking is from bad to worst.

5. At "The Pizza Palace" the crusts are chewy and the sauces are as runny as a runny nose.

4. "The Old Diner" is actually a new restaurant designed to look like a cozy old diner. But it's all fake, except for the food. Most of it tastes like last month's leftovers.

3. The sign outside "100 Different Tacos" brags that they offer the world's largest variety of tacos. What's more amazing is that every one of them is awful.

2. "Something Fishy" is an awful name for a fish restaurant. The phrase means that something is not right. Maybe the owner was being honest, because the food at this restaurant is truly fishy.

1. Finally, the worst restaurant in town is "The Happy Hamburger." Their logo shows a smiling cow. I was not smiling after I took one bite.

Write it: Imagine that you are about to pick a pet for a friend. You go to the pet store and discover that they have only the following pets: a llama, a parrot, a porcupine, a snake, and a tarantula. Rank your top three choices from this group and explain why each made your list.

Hints:
• Before making your choice, list something positive about each animal.
• After choosing the three top pets from the list, write a descriptive title for your article.
• Write a brief introduction to the list.
• Briefly explain why each pet on the list might make your friend happy.

More Ranking Prompts

Write an article that ranks your three favorite sports. Explain what interests you about each sport on your list.

Write an article that ranks your top three heroes. They can be people you know or read about. Tell why each matters to you.

Write an article that ranks your three favorite books. Explain what interests you about each book on your list.

Write an article that ranks your three favorite movies or TV shows. Explain what interests you about each title on your list.

Write an article that ranks the three most important tools that you use. Explain why each tool is important to you.

Write an article that ranks your three favorite places. Explain what interests you about each place on your list.

Scientific Reporting

The word *science* comes from a Latin word meaning "to know" or "to observe." Scientists make observations to satisfy their curiosity or to answer questions, such as "What are the parts of a tooth?" or "How do flies fly?"

"Natural observation" involves studying the subject with as little interference as possible; a famous example is Galileo's first study of the moon using a telescope. "Experimental observation" means controlling the subject to see what happens, for example, limiting the amount of water given to plants to study the effects of drought.

Scientists make detailed reports of what they see so that other scientists can check on the accuracy of the observations.

Model (natural observation)

Galileo's Report on His Moon Observations (1609)

Now let us review the observations made during the past two months, once more inviting the attention of all who are eager for true science. Let us speak first of that surface of the moon which faces us. I distinguish two parts of this surface, a lighter and a darker. The lighter part seems to cover the whole hemisphere, while the darker part appears covered with spots.

Now these spots, which are fairly dark and large, are plain to everyone and have been seen throughout the ages. These are different from others that are smaller in size but so numerous as to occur all over the lunar surface, and especially the lighter part. These small spots had never been seen by anyone before me.

From observations of these spots repeated many times I now believe that the moon's surface is not smooth, uniform, and precisely spherical as many scientists believe it to be, but is uneven and rough, like the face of the earth, relieved by chains of mountains and deep valleys.

Write it: Describe in detail a person's outer ear. This can be done with a mirror; it's easier if you observe someone else's ear.

Hints:
• Include as many facts as you can. Describe the shape, color, and texture of each part. If you have a measuring device, include measurements. You might also make a sketch.
• Include questions inspired by your observation. These questions can be the starting point for further observations.

More Observation Prompts

Describe a process scientifically.
It could be a human activity, for example, walking or running, or an animal activity, for example, the movements of a cat. Give enough information so that other scientists could study the same activity and compare their observations with yours.

Describe part of a plant scientifically.
It could be a fruit, such as a banana or an orange. Or it could be leaf, a flower, a root. Give enough information so that other scientists could study the same object and compare their observations with yours.

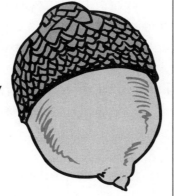

Describe an animal or part of an animal scientifically. It could be an animal found in nature, such as an insect or a bird. Or it could be a domestic animal, such as a cat or a dog. Describe the parts in detail. Give enough information so that other scientists could study the same animal and compare their observations with yours.

Scripting: Adaptation

Dramatic writing involves telling a story through dialogue. Although dramatists often invent original stories for their scripts, many famous scripts are based on older stories.

Model
Original story: "The Rooster and the Ring" by Aesop

A hungry rooster was digging around the barnyard in search of something to eat. From time to time it came upon a grain of corn, which it happily devoured. Suddenly something shiny caught its eye. The rooster looked closer and saw a ring with a huge diamond. The rooster knew the ring was worthless to him. He therefore brushed it aside and kept looking for corn.

Adaptation of "The Rooster and the Ring"

Pig: You sure look busy, Rooster. What in the world are you doing?

Rooster: Looking for something to eat. Ah, there's a grain of corn. Yum.

Pig: I prefer slop myself. But hold on, what's that shiny thing your beak just turned up?

Rooster: Let me see. It's definitely not a piece of corn. Aha. It's a diamond ring.
(The rooster pushes the ring aside and continues hunting for corn.)

Pig: Why did you push the ring aside? It's probably worth a fortune.

Rooster: To a person, maybe, but not to me. I'd rather have one grain of delicious corn than all the diamonds in the world. In my opinion, the worth of something depends on who needs it. I can't use stones, even shiny ones.

Write it: Choose a fable, a myth, a novel, or a story from the newspaper and adapt it as a script. If the story is long, choose one piece of action and turn that part into a script.

Hints:
• Use the script form. Put the character's name before each speech. If you want to describe an action, put that into parentheses. You'll find an example in the model: the rooster pushing the ring aside.

• It's OK to invent new characters or leave out old ones.

• Capture actions by having characters describe what's going on.

More Stories to Adapt

Adapt the following myth or another one as a script.

Daedalus and Icarus

Daedalus was an inventor who lived on the island controlled by King Minos. When the king refused to let Daedalus leave, the inventor created wings for himself and his son Icarus. Daedalus warned Icarus not to fly too high or the sun would melt the wax binding the feathers. But during their escape, Icarus soared far above his father and ignored his warnings. Soon Icarus' wings came apart and the youth fell into the ocean and drowned.

Adapt the following fable or another one as a script.

The Miser and His Gold

A rich man sold all his possessions for a huge bag of gold coins. Fearful that someone would steal the gold, he buried it in the forest. He checked on the gold every day to make sure it was still there. Eventually, a thief, who became curious about the miser's daily trip to the forest, followed the man to the hiding place. The thief returned that night and stole the gold. When the miser complained, a neighbor told him to forget it. The gold hadn't done him any good when he had it.

Adapt the following joke or another one as a script.

A Cheap Room

A traveler asked the innkeeper how much a room would cost. The price was 100 dollars for a room with a bath. When the traveler asked for something cheaper, he was told that there was a room for 50 dollars, but it had no TV. When the traveler said he wanted something cheaper, he was told there was a room for only five dollars, but he would have to make his own bed. He agreed, and the innkeeper handed him wood, nails, and a hammer.

Scripting a Commercial

Creating a radio or TV commercial lets you to practice dramatic writing. You first must come up with a premise (the main action). Then, you invent characters and write the dialogue. The final step is editing the piece to last exactly 60 seconds.

Model

Commercial for Can-Closer

Wife: It's fun preparing a meal together.

Husband: Yeah, but you know what I hate most about cooking?

Wife: Hand me the salt. No, what do you hate most?

Husband: Using only half the stuff in a can, and then having to store it. What a mess.

Wife: That won't be a problem any more. I just bought a Can-Closer.

Husband: What's a Can Closer? I never heard of it.

Wife: The invention of your dreams. When you're ready to reseal a can, just slip the can's lid into the slot at the side of the Can-Closer, put the grooved wheel onto the edge of the can, press the button, and the can is resealed like new. It couldn't be easier.

Husband: Does it really work?

Wife: Try it yourself. Use the Can-Closer to reseal that can of peas you opened earlier.

Sound: Zoom.

Husband: (excited) The Can-Closer really works.

Announcer: The Can-Closer is available for less than twenty dollars at most hardware stores and supermarkets. Or visit our Web site at www.Can-Closer.com.

Write it: Write a 60-second commercial for an automatic dog-feeding machine. You'll need between 150 and 200 words.

Hints:
• Before writing, brainstorm the benefits of owning such a device.
• Decide who your characters will be. Because commercials often are meant to be humorous or fantastical, you could have talking animals as characters. In any case, usually two or three characters will be enough. Often an announcer will make the final speech.
• Decide on your premise. This is the main action. Examples include trying to solve a problem, having an argument, or taking a trip.
• Try to use the product's name at least five times.

More Prompts for Writing Commercials

Write a 60-second commercial for **Bell-Corder:** a doorbell with a built-in recorder. People who drop by when you're not home can leave you a message.

Write a 60-second commercial for **Robo-Pet:** a robot that looks and acts like a domestic animal. Comes in two models: a dog or a cat.

Write a 60-second commercial for **Dry Soap:** a bar of soap that lathers without water. You can use it anywhere.

Write a 60-second commercial for **Sharp-Write:** a pencil that never needs sharpening and never wears down.

Write a 60-second commercial for **Ring Light:** a ring with a built-in miniature but powerful flashlight. You'll never stumble in the dark again.

Write a 60-second commercial for **Tooth Timer:** a toothbrush holder with a clock that automatically measures the amount of time you need to spend brushing.

Sentence Linking

In clear writing, sentences connect securely like links on a chain. You easily can practice linking sentences. Here's how:
1. Write a sentence on any subject that interests you.
2. Circle an important word or phrase in that sentence.
3. Write a follow-up sentence that explains the circled word or phrase in the first sentence.
4. Circle a word or phrase in the second sentence that relates to the circled word or phrase in the first sentence. In some cases this will be the same word or a synonym.
5. Show the link between the sentences by drawing a line between the two circled expressions.

Model

I had a scary (dream) last night. In this (dream,) I was being chased through a dark tunnel by a large (dog.) The (beast) had teeth that flashed on and off like a (neon sign.) I could see the blinking (lights) coming (closer.) If I didn't do something fast, I'd be (caught.) Soon (escape) would be impossible.

Write it: Write your own sentence-linking paragraph. Start with a sentence of your own, or use the following sentence:

Millions of people spend several hours a day watching TV.

Carefully read the first sentence. Look for a word or phrase that you want to build on. It could refer to a person, a place, a thing, or an action. Write a second sentence that says something about the material you circled. Continue until you've added at least four sentences.

Hints:
• Usually, one sentence could be followed up in many ways. There is no one right answer.
• After making several links, you might feel it's time to start a new paragraph. If so, indent the new paragraph and keep adding sentences.

More Prompts for Sentence Linking

Write a series of linked sentences starting with the following sentence. Look for a word or phrase that you want to build on. Write a second sentence that says something about the material you circled. Continue until you've added at least four sentences.

I was lost in the middle of nowhere.

Write a series of linked sentences starting with the following sentence. Look for a word or phrase that you want to build on. Write a second sentence that says something about the material you circled. Continue until you've added at least four sentences.

The silvery rocket rose slowly from its launch pad.

Write a series of linked sentences starting with the following sentence. Look for a word or phrase that you want to build on. Write a second sentence that says something about the material you circled. Continue until you've added at least four sentences.

The huge black bird circled high in the morning sky.

Write a series of linked sentences starting with the following sentence. Look for a word or phrase that you want to build on. Write a second sentence that says something about the material you circled. Continue until you've added at least four sentences.

The human brain is more powerful than any computer.

Write a series of linked sentences starting with the following sentence. Look for a word or phrase that you want to build on. Write a second sentence that says something about the material you circled. Continue until you've added at least four sentences.

Suddenly, all the lights in town went out.

Write a series of linked sentences starting with the following sentence. Look for a word or phrase that you want to build on. Write a second sentence that says something about the material you circled. Continue until you've added at least four sentences.

My life would be very different without books.

More Prompts for Sentence Linking

Write a series of linked sentences starting with the following sentence. Look for a word or phrase that you want to build on. Write a second sentence that says something about the material you circled. Continue until you've added at least four sentences.

It's a good thing plants can't talk.

Write a series of linked sentences starting with the following sentence. Look for a word or phrase that you want to build on. Write a second sentence that says something about the material you circled. Continue until you've added at least four sentences.

The sun has an important effect on Earth.

Write a series of linked sentences starting with the following sentence. Look for a word or phrase that you want to build on. Write a second sentence that says something about the material you circled. Continue until you've added at least four sentences.

The wheel is one of the most important inventions.

Write a series of linked sentences starting with the following sentence. Look for a word or phrase that you want to build on. Write a second sentence that says something about the material you circled. Continue until you've added at least four sentences.

Many people like to watch scary movies.

Write a series of linked sentences starting with the following sentence. Look for a word or phrase that you want to build on. Write a second sentence that says something about the material you circled. Continue until you've added at least four sentences.

Breaking a habit is not easy.

Write a series of linked sentences starting with the following sentence. Look for a word or phrase that you want to build on. Write a second sentence that says something about the material you circled. Continue until you've added at least four sentences.

Hiccups are strange.

More Prompts for Sentence Linking

Write a series of linked sentences starting with the following sentence. Look for a word or phrase that you want to build on. Write a second sentence that says something about the material you circled. Continue until you've added at least four sentences.

What is the best way to prepare for a test?

Write a series of linked sentences starting with the following sentence. Look for a word or phrase that you want to build on. Write a second sentence that says something about the material you circled. Continue until you've added at least four sentences.

Mosquitoes can be a big bother.

Write a series of linked sentences starting with the following sentence. Look for a word or phrase that you want to build on. Write a second sentence that says something about the material you circled. Continue until you've added at least four sentences.

We're lucky that dinosaurs aren't around today.

Write a series of linked sentences starting with the following sentence. Look for a word or phrase that you want to build on. Write a second sentence that says something about the material you circled. Continue until you've added at least four sentences.

Two seconds remained as I prepared to shoot the basketball.

Write a series of linked sentences starting with the following sentence. Look for a word or phrase that you want to build on. Write a second sentence that says something about the material you circled. Continue until you've added at least four sentences.

Some TV commercials are just plain stupid.

Write a series of linked sentences starting with the following sentence. Look for a word or phrase that you want to build on. Write a second sentence that says something about the material you circled. Continue until you've added at least four sentences.

Ahead of us was the tornado.

Simplifying

Writers are sometimes asked to simplify material. For example, a reporter for a popular science magazine may simplify research so that non-scientists can understand new developments.

The challenge is to accurately give the facts while making them easier to understand. This may involve using more familiar synonyms, giving examples, defining words, and shortening sentences. The writer may also reorder information to lead readers from easier to more difficult ideas.

Model

Original material: Photosynthesis is the process by which green plants and some bacteria use light energy to convert water and carbon dioxide into carbohydrates. A light-absorbing pigment, such as chlorophyll, is essential to the process. Chlorophyll gives plants their green color.

Simplified material:

Most animals live by eating green plants or by eating animals that eat plants. But where do the plants get their food? They make it by combining water and carbon dioxide. Carbon dioxide is an invisible gas that is found in our air. Plants breathe in carbon dioxide through their leaves.

The food-making process takes place in the plant's leaves. Light energy is needed for the work to happen. The energy is absorbed by a material called chlorophyll.

Write it: Simplify the following paragraph so that it could be understand by a young child, who would either read it or hear it read aloud.

Steam is an invisible gas produced by boiling water. When steams cools, it turns into a mist called "water vapor," which may be seen above a kettle or in a shower. People call that mist "steam" but the label is not scientifically accurate.

Hints:
• If you're not sure of a word, look it up in a dictionary.
• Think up an interesting introduction, such as a question or a dramatic scene.
• Explain words or facts as you go along. Use examples.

More Prompts to Simplify

Simplify the following paragraph:
    Genetics is the scientific study of heredity. This field grew from Mendel's work on inherited traits, for example, the coloring of a flower. Geneticists found that traits are transmitted by genes, which are found in cells. Each gene contains a code that helps control the construction or function of the organism.

Simplify the following paragraph:
    Nuclear energy is the force stored in the nucleus of an atom and released by splitting the nucleus (called "nuclear fission") or by combining the nucleus of one atom with the nucleus of another atom (called "nuclear fusion"). Nuclear energy was first used in the form of the atom bomb.

Simplify the following paragraph:
    Gravitation, commonly referred to as gravity, is the force that attracts any two particles of matter to each other. In the seventeenth century, Isaac Newton declared that the force that causes objects to fall to earth is also a force that affects the motions of the moon and the planets.

Simplify the following paragraph:
    Vaccination is the injection of a vaccine into a person or an animal to produce disease-fighting antibodies. A vaccine is a weak or nonliving form of a disease-causing microorganism. Vaccines were first used in China, India, and Persia. In the West, Edward Jenner pioneered vaccination to combat cowpox.

Simplify the following paragraph:
    The **Internet** is a collection of computers that are linked together for the purpose of sharing information, such as text, photographs, drawings, music, videos, and interactive experiences. This network makes possible various forms of data exchange, including e-mail.

Simplify the following paragraph:
    A **volcano** is a breach in the crust of a planet through which gases, lava, and ashes, are released. The word, which derives from *Vulcan*, the mythical god of fire, also refers to the mountain built up around the opening by the discharged matter. Volcanoes are categorized as active, dormant, or extinct.

Speculative Writing

No one can be certain what will happen in the future. But scientists and storytellers often try to forecast coming events. Sometimes, this kind of writing focuses on the results that would follow a given event. For example, if the electricity went out for a week, what other events might happen? A composition that describes possibilities is sometimes called "speculative writing." Often, its title begins with the word "If."

Model

If Animals Could Talk

Sometimes I look at my cat and I wonder what she's thinking. If she and I could talk, I would know the answer. I would ask her what she thinks of me and other people, and also if she thinks lions and tigers are her relatives. Being able to talk to my cat and to other animals would probably give me a whole new way of seeing things.

On the other hand, if all animals could talk, this would change my diet. For example, I don't think I'd like to eat chicken if chickens could talk. I'd probably become a vegetarian. Of course, if it turned out that vegetables could talk, I'd be in big trouble.

Other uses of animals might also be a problem. For example, suppose my cat said she didn't want to be my pet. What if she said, "I'd rather live with Sandy across the street." That would definitely make me sad.

Write it: Imagine that people learn to read each other's minds. Write an essay that describes the results of this change.

Hints:
• Think about all sorts of activities that mind reading might affect, for example, games, sports, education, business, friendships, and family relations.
• If you like, include positive and negative consequences.
• Start your essay with a brief introduction that sets the scene.

More Speculative Prompts

Describe what might happen if people could learn everything while sleeping. Think about questions such as "What effect would this have on schools?" and "Would this change libraries?"

Describe what would happen if time travel were possible. Think about questions such as "What historical events would you want to see?" and "What if time travelers changed the past?"

Describe what would happen if all people were equally good at sports. Think about questions such as "Would there still be an Olympics?" and "Would people still watch sports on TV?"

Describe what would happen if babies could talk as soon as they were born. Think about questions such as "What would they say?" and "How would this change family life?"

Describe what would happen if extraterrestrials came from another planet. Think about questions such as "What would the visitors want from us?" and "What could they teach us?"

Describe what would happen if robots did all the work that people now do. Think about questions such as "How would people earn a living?" and "How would people use their time?"

Storytelling: Characters

You can create interesting characters by combining parts from two or more people, animals, or even things. For example, in Greek mythology, the Minotaur had the body of a man and the head of a bull. Before putting your invented creature into a story, write a character sketch about it.

Model

A Skubee

Although a skubee is only the size of a house cat, you don't want to mess with this animal. It is half skunk and half bee, and has the powers of each.

If you ever see a skubee heading your way, you might at first feel like laughing. After all, it isn't every day that you meet a giant striped insect that buzzes as loud as a helicopter.

However, I advise you to stop laughing and to run in the opposite direction as fast as you can. An angry skubee—and most skubees are always angry—will zoom after you and try to blanket you with an awful, smelly liquid. If somehow you are able to avoid the stinky stuff, you are not safe yet. The skubee will next go after you with its long stinger, which is about a foot long and sharp as a sword.

Write it: Imagine a character that combines the features of a whale and an eagle. Give the character a name, and describe what it looks like and how it behaves.

Hints:
• Before writing, list the characteristics of a whale and of an eagle.
• To name your character, you could blend parts of the words *whale* and *eagle* or you could make up a name from scratch.
• Think about how the character might interact with other similar characters or with other characters including people.

More Prompts for Combining Characters

Create a character by combining parts and behaviors from an insect and a person. Insects are six-legged creatures. Examples that you might use include: ant, bee, butterfly, firefly, housefly, and wasp. Make up a name for the character and describe what it looks like and does.

Create a character by combining parts and behaviors of a human and a fish or other water-living animal. Examples include: minnow, goldfish, octopus, porpoise, ray, seal, shark, and whale. Make up a name for the character and describe what it looks like and does.

Create a character by combining parts and behaviors of an amphibian and a person. Amphibians usually start out life as tadpoles and later develop lungs. Examples include: frog, newt, salamander, and toad. Make up a name for the character and describe what it looks like and does.

Create a character by combining parts and behaviors of a human with another mammal. Most mammals are hairy and nurse their young with milk. Examples are: bear, cow, dog, horse, rat, and squirrel. Make up a name for the character and describe what it looks like and does.

Create a character by combining parts and behaviors of a reptile and a person. Reptiles are covered with scales or plates. Examples that you might use include: alligator, crocodile, dinosaur, snake, and turtle. Make up a name for the character and describe what it looks like and does.

Create a character by combining parts and behaviors of any two or more animals. Examples include: crab, elephant, flea, warthog, hummingbird, octopus, rabbit, slug, spider, and tiger. Make up a name for the character and describe what it looks like and does.

Storytelling: Dialogue

Most stories are made up of two kinds of writing: description and dialogue. Dialogue appears inside quotation marks and is the words that characters speak.

Instead of small talk, such as "Hi" or "Nice day," dialogue usually pushes the story along or tells something about the characters. It often involves asking questions, arguing, or revealing secret information. As you read the following model, ask yourself the purpose of each speech.

Model

The Bank Robber

Ruth and I were sitting on a park bench. She was still trying to teach me how to play the harmonica. The instrument screeched.

"You're getting it," she said. "Just be patient."

I wasn't making any progress, but Ruth was always encouraging. Then something caught my eye. I looked and saw Joe Koch run from the bank.

"The bank's being robbed!" he shouted. "You kids run away."

Before we could move, the head teller, Mr. Franz came out of the bank, pushed by a nasty-looking thug whose face was covered by a knit ski mask. The thug had a pistol in one hand and a paper bag in the other.

"He's got the money," I whispered to Ruth, pointing to the bag.

"Nobody move," said the robber, "or someone will get hurt."

Suddenly Ruth's father came running from the other direction.

"Stop," shouted the robber.

Ruth's father said nothing, but somehow I heard the words "Put the gun down. Now." It was mental telepathy, I knew it, but couldn't believe it.

The robber stared at Ruth's father, and slowly lowered the gun.

Write it: Choose a scene from a favorite movie and describe the action mostly in dialogue. Or write an original scene.

Hints:
• Before you write, decide on the main point of the scene.
• Remember to put the spoken words inside quotation marks.
• Add dialogue tags to explain who is talking. A tag can even describe how something is said, for example, the words *shouted* and *whispered*.

More Dialogue Prompts

Argument: Write a scene in which two characters are having an argument. It could be about an opinion (what's the best sport or who's the best writer) or it could be about something that one of the characters did. You could base the scene on something that happened to you.

Questioning: Write a scene in which one character interrogates a second character. This means that the first character asks the second a series of questions. It could be a police officer interrogating a suspect, or it could be a friend trying to get information from another friend. You could base the scene on something that happened to you.

Observation: Write a scene in which the dialogue shows what two characters are seeing. For example, they could be witnessing a flood or a storm. As they talk, the reader gets to "see" what the characters see. You could base the scene on something that happened to you.

Report: Write a scene in which one character reports on an event that happened before the two characters met. For example, the character could describe a stranger who just arrived in town. You could base the scene on something that happened to you.

Plan: Write a scene in which two characters make a plan to do something. It could be something amazing, like building a rocket to go to the moon. Or it could be something ordinary, like throwing a surprise party for a friend. You could base the scene on something that happened to you.

Secret: Write a scene in which one character reveals a secret to another character or makes a confession. Have the character who hears the secret say something that expresses surprise or disbelief. You could base the scene on something that happened to you.

Storytelling: Endings

The ending is one of the most important parts of a story. In fact, writers sometimes create their endings first, and then write the rest of the story. For example, suppose you wrote the following ending: "I was sure glad that the bag of gold was gone." Could you invent a story leading to that final line?

Model

Good-bye, Gold

A friend and I were walking through a park when I saw a bag under a bush. I planned to throw the bag into the litter bin, but when I looked inside, I saw two bars of gold.

I said, "I'm going to call the police. They'll find the owner."

"Are you serious?" said my friend. "The gold is worth thousands of dollars. If you don't want it, I'll take it." My friend tried to grab the bag, but I held on and ran away. Soon everyone in my neighborhood was after me. Luckily, I'm a fast runner and escaped.

I hid in a garage where I found a portable radio. I clicked it on and heard a news flash about "a stupid kid who planned to give back a million dollars' worth of gold." A million dollars! That's how rumors grow. If I didn't do something fast, it might soon be a billion.

I sneaked off and ran to the river. It was dark by then. I flung the bag as far as I could into the water and watched it sink. I smiled knowing that if I had kept the gold, everyone would have wanted it. Now I'd be teased for a few days. Then the incident would be forgotten. I was sure glad that the bag of gold was gone.

Write it: Write a story that ends with the following line:
   I would never read another person's mind again.

Hints:
• Before writing, list a few problems that might happen if you could read other people's minds.
• Before writing, list the main characters for your story.
• Before writing, imagine a dramatic opening scene for your story.
• Before writing, think up a "working title" for your story. This is a preliminary title. You can always change it after you've written the story.

More Ending Prompts

Write a short story that <u>ends</u> with the following line:
    The cat would never chase a mouse again.

Write a short story that <u>ends</u> with the following line:
    Now I understood why I had always liked robots more than people.

Write a short story that <u>ends</u> with the following line:
    The stranger smiled for the first time.

Write a short story that <u>ends</u> with the following line:
    I set the dial of the time machine back 150 years and pressed "Go."

Write a short story that <u>ends</u> with the following line:
    I answered, "I'm moving to Mars."

Write a short story that <u>ends</u> with the following line:
    Now I knew for sure: Two heads *are* better than one.

Write a short story that <u>ends</u> with the following line:
    She took the huge diamond from her pocket and gave it to the little boy.

Write a short story that <u>ends</u> with the following line:
    The only problem was: How do you hide a whale?

More Ending Prompts

Write a short story that <u>ends</u> with the following line:
I smashed that dream-making machine into a thousand pieces.

Write a short story that <u>ends</u> with the following line:
I learned one thing from the experience: Spaghetti can be dangerous.

Write a short story that <u>ends</u> with the following line:
I stopped shrinking when I reached the size of a grain of sand. I was exactly the size I wanted to be.

Write a short story that <u>ends</u> with the following line:
It was snowing hard in the desert, but no one even noticed.

Write a short story that <u>ends</u> with the following line:
"You'll be sorry," threatened the extraterrestrial, but I just grinned.

Write a short story that <u>ends</u> with the following line:
The secret would stay a secret inside me for the rest of my life.

Write a short story that <u>ends</u> with the following line:
What a choice—to become a tomato or an onion. I thought for a moment and then said, "Tomato."

Write a short story that <u>ends</u> with the following line:
The phone rang, but I didn't answer it.

More Ending Prompts

Write a short story that <u>ends</u> with this scene:

Write a short story that <u>ends</u> with this scene:

Write a short story that <u>ends</u> with this scene:

Write a short story that <u>ends</u> with this scene:

Write a short story that <u>ends</u> with this scene:

Write a short story that <u>ends</u> with this scene:

Storytelling: Finding Plots

Writers often find story ideas in the news. They might change names, add or drop details, and make up a new ending.

Model

The story below was based on the following newspaper article:

A fortune-teller gazed at a client's palm and told the man that he would soon get money. A few days later, the man returned with a knife and then took the fortune-teller's jewelry and her purse, which contained more than one hundred dollars in cash. The man escaped before police arrived.

The Fortune-teller's Future

Madame Futura studied the palm of a man who sat before her. "You are worried," she said, "because you can't pay your bills."

The man said nothing. The only sound was laughter from people walking on the carnival midway outside Madame Futura's tent.

The fortune-teller smiled and said soothingly, "Do not be concerned. You will soon come into riches."

With that, the man pulled a knife from his pocket. "I will," he replied, "if you have a lot of money in that purse of yours. Hand it over."

Madame Futura obeyed. The man took the purse and turned to leave. "I advise you to look into your future," said Madame Futura. "I see trouble ahead for you."

The thief looked back and said, "And I advise you to pay more attention to your own future." Then he was gone.

Write it: Turn the following article into a story or a scene.

A woman heard scratching at her back door and opened it, thinking she was about to let in her pet cat. Instead, two huge lions entered. The woman fled out the front door and jumped on her bicycle and was able to outdistance the lions. Later, she learned that the lions had escaped from a circus.

Hints:
• Before you write, think up a title.
• Give the characters names.
• Add dialogue.
• Change whatever details you like, and think up a real ending.

More Newspaper Plot Prompts

A military exercise nearly ended in tragedy. The troops ambushed a group of hunters. Thinking they were military personnel masquerading as the enemy, the troops fired blanks at the hunters. But the hunters, thinking that they were being attacked by criminals, returned the fire with live ammunition. Luckily no one was hurt.

An English teen, who wanted to see the world, hid aboard a ship that he thought was bound for distant ports. A day later the boy came out, believing it would be too late for the boat to turn around. However, he discovered that the ship had moved only a short distance to another part of the harbor where it was undergoing repairs.

A car thief used a rope to tow a small sports car out of a driveway. The car sped up and rolled over the thief's foot. It then pinned the thief against a wall. The car's owner, didn't know what was happening until he heard the sound of a car horn. The owner looked outside and saw that the thief was honking for help.

A man whose home was drafty cut open his living room floor to try to locate the source of the cold air. He discovered a 1,000 foot (330 meter) deep cavity. He and his family moved their belongings out of the room and called the authorities. Experts later determined that the house had been built above a two-century-old mine shaft.

A man hijacked a yacht at a wharf, put the owner ashore, and guided the boat out of the harbor and into the ocean. However, a few hours later, the hijacker became violently seasick. He radioed for help and was eventually towed ashore by authorities who then arrested him. The boat was undamaged.

An undertaker heard snoring from the coffin containing an 85-year-old woman, who had been pronounced dead by a physician. The coffin had been brought to the chapel for a service. The undertaker opened the coffin and discovered that the woman was very much alive. She was rushed to a hospital where she was said to be doing well.

Storytelling: Recycled Plots

A retold story twists the ending of an earlier story, often in a humorous way. Such stories are sometimes known as "parodies."

Model
Broadway Bound

The wolf saw Little Red Riding Hood carrying goodies to Grandma Hood and came up with a plan. He hurried to Grandma's house and ate her all up. But he didn't chew so she wasn't hurt.

Soon, Little Red arrived and saw someone in Grandma's bed, dressed in Grandma's outfit. Little Red Riding Hood was sure it was not Grandma. In order to find out who it was, she decided to play along.

"Grandma," she said, "what big eyes you have."

"The better to see you with, my dear," said the figure in the bed. That was more evidence that this wasn't Grandma, whose eyesight was failing.

"Grandma," said Little Red, "what big ears you have."

"The better to hear you with, my dear." That was also suspicious because Grandma always said that Little Red talked too much.

"And Grandma, what big teeth you have."

The wolf knew he had been discovered and leaped from the bed in order to catch and devour Little Red. But before he could do so, she started to applaud.

"What's that for?" he asked.

"You are a wonderful actor," she said. "You almost made me think you were Grandma. You could be a big star if you spent time practicing."

"Can you help me?" he asked.

"Sure," she said, "if you give back Grandma."

Instantly, the wolf coughed up Grandma, who was in perfect condition. True to her word, Little Red Riding Hood coached the wolf, who will soon be starring in a movie.

Write it: Retell the same story, giving it a completely different twist.

Hints:
- It's OK to change the beginning of your version.
- You can add or drop characters.
- Give your version a new name.

More Prompts for Retelling

Retell the following story:

Two kids are abandoned in the woods. They come across a house made of candy. They enter seeking help. The owner tries to capture and cook them for dinner. They outwit her and escape. When the woman chases the kids, they use magic to turn stones into bread. She eats the phony bread, which turns back into stones while she's swimming after the kids, and she drowns.

Retell the following story:

A girl hiking through the woods comes across a house that is furnished, but nobody is home at the moment. The girl enters the house without permission and eats the owners' food, tries out their furniture, and falls asleep. When the owners return—they are a family of bears—the bears chase the girl away.

Retell the following story:

A boy's mom sends him to the market to sell their cow. Instead, the boy trades the cow for a handful of beans. The mother throws the beans out the window. One bean grows into a stalk that reaches the sky. The boy climbs the stalk, enters a giant's house, steals a valuable goose, and escapes down the stalk, which he chops down in order to kill the giant, who is chasing him.

Summarizing a Story

"Summarizing" means using a few words to capture the main idea of a piece of writing. This skill has many uses. For example, when you review a novel or a movie, you may sum up the plot.

Model

The Eagle and the Fox: An Aesop Fable

While hunting for food for her chicks, an eagle saw a fox's cub in a field. As the eagle grasped the cub, the cub's mother arrived and begged the eagle to set the cub free. The eagle replied, "I'll do no such thing. My chicks are hungry. But let me give you some advice. Never beg. It just makes you seem like a weakling."

With that she flew to her nest atop a nearby oak, feeling safe because foxes can't climb. But the mother fox ran to a campfire, took a flaming stick in her mouth, and carried it to the trunk of the oak. The eagle saw that the fox intended to burn the tree and kill the chicks.

"Stop," begged the eagle. "I'll free your cub if you let my chicks live." The fox dropped the stick and the eagle returned the cub.

Summary of "The Eagle and the Fox"

When an eagle grabs a fox cub, the mother fox uses her wits to free her cub and teach the eagle a lesson.

Write it: Summarize the following fable in 30 or fewer words.

A lion saw four bulls living together in a field. The lion said to himself, "I can't attack them. As a group, they could kill me."

After thinking about his problem, the lion came up with a plan. He told other animals rumors about each of the bulls, for example, saying that one bull thought the others were stupid. The lion told these tales as if he had heard each from one bull or another.

The bulls heard the rumors and became so angry at each other, they moved to distant parts of the field. The lion now attacked each one separately, and eventually ate them all up.

Hints:
• Before writing, read the story several times so that you know it well.
• When you draft your summary, skip every other line to leave room for cutting words and rearranging your text.

More Prompts for Summarizing

Summarize the following tall tale in 30 or fewer words.

A kid I know runs so fast no one wants to race him. I told him, "What's the use? No one can keep up with you." That gave him an idea. He turned to his shadow and said, "Let's race to the end of the block and back."

The shadow agreed. The race began. The kid ran like a laser leaving his shadow behind. The shadow stopped and said something to a horse that was watching. The horse nodded, and the shadow climbed onto the horse's shadow and won the race. The kid complained that his shadow had cheated. What a bad loser.

Summarize the following tall tale in 30 or fewer words.

A few years ago, I found a dinosaur egg. Don't ask me how I knew it was a dinosaur egg. OK, ask me.

"How did you know it was a dinosaur egg?"

Simple. The egg was labeled "Jupoptrexus." And I knew for sure that's what it was.

"How did you know for sure?" you're thinking. "Maybe the egg was mislabeled."

I know it wasn't because its mother was sitting on the egg. That's why I didn't bring back the egg. Mother dinosaurs don't like to give up their eggs.

Summarize the following tall tale in 30 or fewer words.

My cousin was always bragging about her parrot. The bird was amazing. It could say about 100 words, but none longer than four syllables.

I decided I'd teach my dog to talk. That would show my cousin a thing or two. In six months the dog could chatter away. His specialty was knock knock jokes.

My cousin was astounded. I took the dog to a TV agent. But after the agent listened a while, he said, "We don't need comedians. If the dog could sing, then we could use him."

Titling a Piece of Writing

Creating an interesting title is the first step in capturing a reader's interest. A memorable title usually focuses on the most important element in the writing. The title often focuses on a character, for example, *Tuck Everlasting*, or on an event, for example, *The War of the Worlds*, or on a place, for example, *Where the Wild Things Are*.

To create a memorable title, a writer will usually begin by brainstorming many possible titles. The next step is evaluating each title and choosing the one that works best.

One way to practice writing titles is to think up a new name for an old story.

Model
Retitle "The Three Little Pigs"

Possible titles:
1. How the Pigs Outsmarted the Wolf
2. There's a Wolf on the Roof
3. The Wolf's Big Threat
4. What to Do When Someone Promises to Blow Your House Down
5. The War Between the Wolf and the Pigs

Choice: I prefer "There's a Wolf on the Roof" because it creates an unusual picture. You don't usually see a wolf on a roof. The idea of a wolf being up there will make the reader want to know more.

"How the Pigs Outsmarted the Wolf" tells too much. It doesn't leave anything to the imagination.

"The Wolf's Big Threat" doesn't relate enough to the action. He does make a threat, but that's just talk. The real action happens when he decides to come down the chimney.

Title 4 is too long, and title 5 isn't right since there isn't a war.

Write it: Write a new title for "Cinderella."

Hints:
• Before writing, think about the main characters and actions.
• While brainstorming, write down all your thoughts. Sometimes a weak idea will lead you to a stronger one.
• Play with word sounds, including rhymes and alliteration.

More Title Prompts

Write a new title for a famous fairy tale. It could be "Hansel and Gretel," "Sleeping Beauty," or another classic. Brainstorm at least five possible titles. Then choose the one you like best. Finally, write a paragraph that explains why you like the title you chose. Also explain weaknesses that you found in the other titles.

Write a new title for a TV series. It could be *Sesame Street*, *The X-Files*, *Third Rock from the Sun*, or any other popular program. Brainstorm at least five possible titles. Then choose the one you like best. Finally, write a paragraph that explains why you like the title you chose. Also explain weaknesses that you found in the other titles.

Write a new title for a movie. It could be *E.T.*, *The Lion King*, *The Wizard of Oz*, *Titanic*, or any other well-known film. Brainstorm at least five possible titles. Then choose the one you like best. Finally, write a paragraph that explains why you like the title you chose. Also explain weaknesses that you found in the other titles.

Write a new title for a comic strip. It could be *Peanuts*, *Blondie*, *Beetle Bailey*, *Garfield*, *Cathy*, *Doonesbury*, or any other popular series. Brainstorm at least five possible titles. Then choose the one you like best. Finally, write a paragraph that explains why you like the title you chose. Also explain weaknesses that you found in the other titles.

Write a new title for a novel. It could be *Little House on the Prairie*, *Treasure Island*, or any other well-known book. Brainstorm at least five possible titles. Then choose the one you like best. Finally, write a paragraph that explains why you like the title you chose. Also explain weaknesses that you found in the other titles.

Write a new title for a song. It could be a current hit or an old favorite, such as "Clementine," or "Waltzing Matilda." Brainstorm at least five possible titles. Then choose the one you like best. Finally, write a paragraph that explains why you like the title you chose. Also explain weaknesses that you found in the other titles.

Classroom Management

Strategies for Quality Practice

Practice does have a payoff if done correctly. To provide quality practice for your student writers, consider the following ideas:

1. Be sure students know why they're practicing. The goal is to become skillful, not just do the activity. Sharing a goal can be as simple as saying: "We're practicing dialogue today because you'll use it in your short story writing project next week."

2. Make students aware that the practice contributes to classroom achievement. For example, the prompts in this book are designed to help students develop frequently used skills.

3. Give attention to timing. If a concept is new, schedule practices close together. Later, spread out the practices, returning to previous prompts for a refresher session that reinforces learning.

4. Keep practice sessions short. It's much better to leave students wanting more.

5. Vary the experience. This starts with content: covering many skills and applications. But it also involves having students sometimes practice solo and sometimes practice in small groups.

6. Actively involve students by building on what they know. For example, in the humor-through-puns practice, you might have students discuss examples heard in movies, such as *Airplane*.

7. Encourage collaboration. Sharing knowledge and experiences builds individual confidence and a sense of community.

8. Provide models to remove guesswork from practice. Each lesson in this book features a model. Add your own models by demonstrating a practice at the board while students watch.

9. Never grade practice. The goal is to learn from mistakes and to build positive habits. Evaluation comes after sufficient practice, when students apply what they learned, for example, by writing short stories for publication. (Mark a "P" at the top of practice papers to differentiate practice from other types of work.)

10. Arrange for encouraging, instructive feedback. Allow students to self-correct and improve their work. This can be done in one-on-one conferences or with large groups.

Independent Writing Center

After introducing a skill such as personification, you may decide that students need additional practice. This can be efficiently carried out in a classroom writing center using the learning cards found on the "More Prompts" page.

Depending on available space, your writing center can be as simple as a table used occasionally for independent work. Another option is to create a permanent writing center stocked with a variety of writing and publishing materials, such as a dictionary, a thesaurus, a style guide, a computer, and book-binding resources.

In the center, you can have students work with the learning cards found on the "More Prompts" pages following the key lessons. You might duplicate and laminate each page, then cut out the cards, and store them in a file-card box or even in a shoe box.

If you would like to offer students more support with their independent practice, you can easily create Power Prompt Practice Folders using ordinary manila file folders and the "More Prompts" learning cards. (See next page.)

Power Prompt Practice Folder

Materials
- file folder
- business-size envelope
- copy of a prompt
- a laminated model of the type of writing to be practiced (This can be teacher-written or duplicated from the key lesson.)

Divide the open file folder into four sections.

In section 1, glue or tape a copy of the learning card.

In section 2, write suggestions or questions that provide the student with additional prewriting ideas. When independent writing is undeveloped, it is often because the independent writer does not do enough thinking, planning, or research before beginning to write.

In section 3, list the steps for doing the practice. For example:
A. Read the laminated model.
B. Draft your work. Remember to double-space so that you can edit it later.
C. Review your draft and make any changes that are needed.
D. Sign up for an editing conference. We will use the same criteria that were used with the introductory practice.
E. Decide if you want to share your work with others either by posting it or reading it in a small group.

In section 4, glue the business envelope and label it "Tips." Add a note such as: "When you are finished, please write a suggestion for other students using this prompt. Place your tip in the envelope."

Enclose the laminated model in the folder.

Number and name the prompt practice on the tab. This will facilitate filing and management.

Place the prompt practice folders in a box in the writing center.

Creating Models

Student writers need to read models. Literary examples help students structure their own ideas. That's why models are included with all the key lessons in this book, and why we suggest that you write additional models for the Power Prompt Practice Folders described on the previous page.

When creating your own models, or adapting those found in the book, write them at the independent reading level of your class. For the models to serve their purpose, they should be easy to read. Rather than struggle with comprehension, students should focus on the structural elements of the assignment.

To build interest we recommend that you personalize the content, for example, by including references to places and events related to your town. Specifically, you might work in:
• student names
• the school name
• your name
• the names of the principal, the bus driver, and other staff
• class pets
• areas or items in the classroom
• experiences that the class has shared, such as fire drills or field trips
• topics and facts from class units
• names and locales from favorite stories
• favorite class games
• class rules
• favorite recess activities
• favorite television characters
• people or events students know from history

One final source of models should be mentioned: In doing the exercises, students will often create manuscripts that, with a little editing, can serve as models in future years. When we find suitable examples, we ask students if we can keep copies of their work for this purpose. Almost always, students are delighted to contribute to the classroom's learning resources.

Developing Editing Criteria

Writing doesn't stop with a first draft. Even when students do a short ten-minute exercise, set aside time to edit the draft.

Editing should be done first by the student writer. When time permits, much will be gained from a follow-up editing conference involving the teacher or—after training—a classmate. (See the next page for tips on structuring editing conferences.) Whether the editing is done solo or with the assistance of an editor, it should always cover two areas: content and mechanics.

Content includes ideas, wording, and format requirements. For example, if the assignment calls for using a simile, the piece should include a simile. During content editing, students may:
• delete extraneous material
• add missing material
• rearrange the elements for clarity or interest
• improve word choice
• check facts

Mechanics covers sentence variety, grammar, punctuation, paragraphing, and spelling. During mechanics editing, students may:
• combine or divide sentences
• clarify pronoun references
• correct subject/verb problems
• correct spelling errors
• insert paragraph breaks or combine paragraphs

Editing time is often limited when doing prompt-style practices. Thus, we find it more productive to focus on a few issues rather than have students edit "for everything" as might be done with a major writing project. When deciding which few criteria to use for a given exercise, consider the following:
• the focus of the prompt: If the exercise is about comparing and contrasting, students should make sure that the draft compares and contrasts two subjects.
• problems that you have noted in previous assignments
• standards or requirements mandated by your school or district

For balance, include both content and mechanics criteria. If you focus entirely on mechanics, students may undervalue ideas.

A Helpful Feedback Conference

Giving feedback to young writers can be tricky. Students who feel that completing a draft is sufficient may not welcome editorial comments. To change that counterproductive mind set, we have developed a four-step routine known as

Read S.A.S.

Before an editing conference, the teacher reads the student's work and makes notes based on the content and mechanics. Also, the teacher may ask the student to write preliminary comments about his or her draft. (See the Editing Conference Preparation Sheet, next page.) The steps of "Read S.A.S." follow:

Step 1. Read. The feedback conference begins with an oral reading, sometimes by the writer and sometimes by the editor. The entire work may be read, but much can be accomplished if—given time limits—the student chooses an excerpt.

Step 2. Find the **S**trengths. The teacher identifies what works in the piece. This includes comments on elements that satisfy the listed criteria ("You were supposed to include descriptive dialogue, and I see half a dozen good examples") as well as notes on general strengths ("You used many specific verbs, and not a single cliché").

Step 3. Ask questions. There is no better way to show interest in a writer's work. You can focus on the writing process ("What kind of research did you do to find out about the construction of the pyramids?"). Or you can zero in on an element in the manuscript ("How do you feel about using the second person point of view compared with using the first person?").

Step 4. Suggest ways to improve the piece. But do so only after asking if the student is ready to hear your ideas. No use giving advice if the writer doesn't want to listen.

Assuming that the student is open to suggestions, use the content and mechanics criteria list to identify areas that need improvement. Either the teacher or the student can make notes during this step so that there is a written record of the editing work to be done.

For ways to publish work after it is polished, see "Ideas for Sharing Writing" later in this section.

Editing Conference Preparation Sheet

Fill out and attach this paper to your draft. If you need more space to answer questions, use the back of this sheet or another piece of paper.

Writer's name _____

Prompt focus (description, dialogue, etc.) _____

Title of work _____ Date _____

1. In your own words, briefly define the focus of the prompt.

_____

_____

2. What do you like best about what you wrote, and why?

_____

_____

3. What part do you like least, and why?

_____

_____

4. What did you learn while writing this assignment?

_____

_____

5. What changes did you make when editing the draft?

_____

_____

6. In the draft, circle a sentence that you think is especially strong. Tell what you like about the sentence.

_____

_____

7. What questions do you have about the assignment? Was there any part of it that puzzled you or that was difficult?

_____

_____

Ideas for Sharing Writing

Publishing student work has many benefits. It:
• reinforces the idea of writing for an audience
• helps the student writer discover his/her own voice
• increases student concern for editing and "getting it right"
• serves as a reward for making a big effort
• creates a record of student writing
• enables teacher and student to monitor progress through the year

Here are some simple ways to share writing:

• Dedicate a bulletin board to prompt-inspired manuscripts. Use easy-to-remove tacks so that students can easily take a piece down, read it, and then return it.

• Hang manuscripts from a mobile.

• Collect work in a notebook and make the notebook available to parents at conferences.

• Arrange for oral presentations in small groups or for the whole class. Most students enjoy hearing their work read aloud by a classmate or by the teacher, but this should be done only with the writer's permission.

• Make a "radio program" of work read onto audiotape.

• Create a class yearbook, with each student choosing and submitting a piece. This book might then be read by students in future years.

• Each week feature one prompt-inspired piece in the class newspaper.

• Make individual portfolios of prompt-inspired pieces so that students can review their work from time to time.

• Make a class book of many versions of the same assignment.

• Adapt a piece of writing as a reader's theater script.

• Publish work on the classroom or school Web site.

Language Scouting for Models

Students benefit in three ways from studying literary models. First, models suggest ideas to write about. Second, they illustrate techniques, such as comparing and contrasting. Third, models teach structure, for example, how a story is put together. For these reasons, a model is included with each Power Prompt lesson.

To expand this collection of models and to strengthen the connection between skill practices and real-world writing, try an activity called *language scouting*. Students comb through books, magazines, newspapers, poetry, directions, even advertisements, looking for examples of analogies, persuasive writing, paraphrasing, and so on.

After finding an item, a student should copy it onto a piece of paper (or attach a clipping), name the source, and identify the technique illustrated (for example, "humor through exaggeration"). The student may then share the model orally or post it on a bulletin board.

To prepare students for real-world language scouting, try the activity using the ready-made "clippings" on the following page:
• *The Perfect Storm*: descriptive writing (with sound and smell)
• *Lives of a Cell*: comparing
• *Tuesdays with Morrie*: listing
• e-mail letter: comparing, speculative writing, second-person point of view
• newspaper sports article: humor through exaggeration, personification
• letter to the editor: comparing and contrasting, second-person point of view, titling

Give each student, or a small group, the handout. Then see which techniques the students can spot on their own.

Clippings for Language Scouting Practice

from *The Perfect Storm* by Sebastian Junger, page 5

A soft fall rain slips down through the trees and the smell of ocean is so strong that it can almost be licked off the air. Trucks rumble along Rogers Street and men in t-shirts stained with fishblood shout to each other from the decks of boats.

from *The Lives of a Cell* by Lewis Thomas, page 75

Working a typewriter by touch, like riding a bicycle or strolling on a path, is best done by not giving it a glancing thought. Once you do, your fingers fumble and hit the wrong keys.

from *Tuesdays with Morrie* by Mitch Albom, page 14

My dream was to be a famous musician (I played the piano), but after several years of dark, empty nightclubs, broken promises, bands that kept breaking up and producers who seemed excited about everyone but me, the dream soured.

from an e-mail sent by a friend

It's a miracle that I am answering your e-mail. Our house is being remodeled. Nothing is where it should be. The place looks as if a tornado blew through it. The refrigerator is in the living room. My bed is in the hall. Chairs are stacked upside down in the bathroom. All our clothing is in suitcases or cardboard boxes.

I spent about four hours trying to find my computer so that I could send you this e-mail. Actually, I don't know exactly how many hours it took because all the clocks have been removed from the walls. Even my wristwatch is missing. What a mess.

Maybe 100 years in the future people won't go through this sort of thing. I can imagine people living in virtual houses. If you want an indoor swimming pool in your basement, you'll type a command, and the pool will appear. You won't actually jump into it, but by wearing a virtual suit, you'll get the feeling you are swimming.

With a keystroke you could change the colors of the walls or the scenes outside the windows. If you wanted to live on the moon, no problem. Just tell the computer and that's what you'd get. At least, it would seem that way to you.

I read an article about virtual reality. I wish I could send it to you. It's here somewhere. But it would take me a year to find it.

Clipping for Language Scouting Practice

from a newspaper sports section

Rattlers Sting Bulldogs

Yesterday, the basketball season opened with a game between the visiting Rattlers and our own Bulldogs. The final score—Rattlers 108, Bulldogs 7—doesn't tell the real story. Bulldog fans may not want the real the story. But my job is to write it. If you don't want to read it, turn the page.

This was the worst loss in history. I don't mean just in basketball. This was worse than what happened to Napoleon at Waterloo. This was worse than what happened to Earth in *War of the Worlds*.

The Rattlers scored the first 55 points. They shot the ball in with one hand. They shot with one finger. They shot the ball just by looking at it. They shot the ball by thinking about it. No matter how they shot it, you'd hear a whoosh as the ball jetted toward the basket, then a kabunk as it hit the backboard and ricocheted through the hoop, or a boing as it hit the rim and dropped down.

It didn't matter where the Rattlers shot from. Sometimes they were under the basket. Sometimes they were at the far end of the court. A few times, they were outside the gym. They could have been on the moon. The told the ball, "Go in," and it replied, "OK." Everyone on the Rattlers team scored at least 8 points.

On the other hand, our Bulldogs didn't score a point until the last minute of the first half. No Bulldog got more than 2 points. The players could have been on a ladder right above the basket, and still they wouldn't have scored.

The Bulldogs didn't know that the idea is to shoot the ball through the hoop. They looked at the ball as if it were a strange object from another planet. When they tried to bounce or pass the ball, usually it went off a foot or directly into the Rattler's basket. But once it did go to a Bulldog cheerleader. Maybe that should count for something.

After the Rattlers built an 80-point lead, their scoring slowed a bit. Maybe their arms got tired. Or maybe they felt sorry for our side. In any case, they started shooting with their eyes closed, but even then, the ball usually went in. Perhaps the Rattlers should have played with only four players, or three, or none. Yes, that would have given us a chance: five of ours against none of theirs. We still wouldn't have scored much, but at least the Rattlers would have stopped making baskets.

Clipping for Language Scouting Practice

from a newspaper letters column

Your editorial entitled "Let's Go to Mars!" said that settling the red planet would be like colonizing America centuries ago. But your comparison does not hold up. You also said it would be exciting. I couldn't agree less.

For one thing, transporting settlers from Europe to America was inexpensive, whereas moving astronauts to another planet will be extremely costly. Who will pay for it? What needed programs on Earth will be cut? Who will benefit? Who will lose out?

For another, when the colonists arrived in America, they found a treasure chest of natural resources including food, water, wood, and wildlife. Because Mars contains few resources, the basics will have to be shipped there.

As for the project being fun, I don't think so. Put yourself into the astronauts' shoes. After blasting off, you'll travel in space for nearly a year in cramped quarters that would make a prison cell seem positively comfortable. You'll eat frozen or artificial food. Water will be scarce, so you won't take showers. You'll never see a rainbow (except on a video), nor go swimming, nor do any other activities that most people enjoy.

There will be only eight colonists on board. If you happen to become unfriendly with one of them, too bad. You won't be able to avoid them or move away. You'll be trapped with no escape.

Meanwhile, every minute you'll worry about being hit by a meteorite. If you hit one, you won't have other things to worry about.

If you do make it to Mars, that's where the real "fun" begins: walking around in a big, bulky spacesuit, doing scientific experiments that could be done better by a robot, and wishing you were home on Earth, skiing or surfing or doing whatever Earthlings do. But wishing won't help. You'll be a sad Martian.

If I were writing an editorial on this subject, I would have called it "Let's Stay at Home and Make Things Better for All of Us."

J. K. Ogenthor

Format Lessons

The lessons in *Power Prompts* focus on techniques used in all sorts of assignments. For example, persuasive writing might be included in a letter to the editor or in a campaign speech, or in a story in which one character tries to fool another. (The opening of *Tom Sawyer* is a famous example.)

In *Power Prompts,* most of the exercises ask students to practice by writing in one of three familiar forms: the essay, the story, or the report. To help students understand the nuts and bolts of these fundamental forms, you might use the teaching steps listed below along with the handouts on the following three pages. To introduce students to a wider variety of formats, you might look at our earlier book, *How to Teach Writing Without Going Crazy.* It covers several dozen formats.

General Method for Teaching Any Format

1. Read models. In addition to having students read the models, read aloud one or two. The ear is a powerful teaching aid.

2. Analyze the models. Help students recognize the elements that make up the format. When teaching the story, for example, this includes pointing out the main characters (protagonist, antagonist); the dialogue; the narration; the setting; and the plot points (trigger event, main conflict, climax).

3. Give a step-by-step recipe. This is a set of directions that provides a method for producing a work.

4. Demonstrate the recipe. The most powerful lesson is for the teacher to write on the board or on the overhead projector as students watch.

5. Make the first assignment short. This way students can focus on getting the elements right, rather than on quantity.

6. Evaluate the results. Always relate the work to the elements covered in the recipe. For example, you might ask students to identify the *trigger events* and *climaxes* in their stories.

7. Try again. Repetition is essential. One time is not enough to master writing letters, lyrics, memoirs, or any other form.

Essay

The essay is a nonfiction work that usually combines facts, opinions, and descriptions. The typical subject is personal, for example, a painful or joyful experience. The style tends to be conversational. The goal is to involve the reader in the subject.

In writing an essay, the following steps are commonly followed.

1. Choose a subject. It should be something that interests you.

2. Find your main idea. This is called the theme or message. An example would be, "Eating pizza is best done with friends." Often, the main idea is captured in the title.

3. Brainstorm a few important points. These might be examples, anecdotes, or facts. You don't have to use them all when you write the essay, but it's useful to have them handy.

4. Form a plan. Some essayists write a detailed outline. Others make a simple list of topics. You can change your plan later, but having one before you start can push you in the right direction.

5. Think up an interesting lead. The lead (pronounced "leed") is the opening sentence or paragraph. Its purpose is to grab the reader's interest. The lead may consist of a surprising fact, an intriguing question, a dramatic description, or a bold statement, for example, "I'll never eat ice cream again."

6. Draft the essay. Use an informal tone. Imagine that you are talking to your reader.

7. Look for a strong ending. This might be a final argument, or a convincing example. Frequently, the ending echoes back to what was said in the lead.

8. Edit the essay. This starts with a careful reading of the manuscript. Try reading it aloud. Look for weak spots: irrelevant ideas, repetitions, inaccuracies. Make changes for the sake of clarity and conciseness.

9. Test the essay with a trial reader. Ask for feedback. Then revise your essay if you find ways to improve it.

Story (Fiction)

A story tells about events that happen in the writer's imagination. This is so even if the inspiration comes from a real event, such as the sinking of the *Titanic*.

1. Pick a subject. Most stories grow from a character (the James Bond series); a problem (a flood, an asteroid heading to Earth); or a belief (for example, that truth is a great value).

2. Figure out the main idea. Often, this can be done in a sentence or two, for example, "A girl follows a rabbit underground and has a series of wonderful adventures."

3. Choose a narrator. This is the person who tells the story. Of course, the writer is really the storyteller, but writers often choose to speak through a character. (This is called a first-person story.)

4. Describe the main characters. You can write a long biography of your main characters, but often a few words will do:
• a hungry, sneaky wolf
• two lazy pig brothers
• a third pig brother, who is sensible, hard working, and clever

5. Outline the plot. The plot consists of the story's major events in the order that they happen. Early in the plot, a trigger event may cause a problem for the main character. Other important events in a plot are the main struggle, such as a fight or an escape; and the climax (when the story's main conflict or problem is resolved).

6. Draft the story. Find a way to make the beginning and ending dramatic. To build interest, have characters describe the settings and the actions. Hint: Writers often change their outlines in the drafting step.

7. Edit the story. First, read it carefully to yourself. See if the actions flow smoothly from start to finish. Is the dialogue interesting and are the characters believable? Polish the wording. Check the spelling and punctuation.

8. Test the story with a trial reader. Ask for feedback. Then revise your story if you find ways to improve it.

Report (Based on Research)

A report gives readers information about a subject. The facts may come from firsthand research, for example, an experiment that the writer carried out. Or the facts can come from books or other secondhand sources.

1. Pick a subject. It should be something that interests you.

2. Brainstorm questions about your subject. For example, if you're going to write about flies, you might ask:
• Are they dirty?
• Do they do any good for people—the way bees make honey?
• Are they intelligent?
If you can't think of any interesting questions about your subject, try reading a short book or an encyclopedia article about it. This is called "background reading" and it usually will inspire questions.

3. Choose one big question to focus on. It should be a question whose answer you don't know.

4. Gather information on the subject. This is called "doing research." If you are taking information from books, write each important fact on a separate note card with the name of the book or source where you found the fact. If you are doing an experiment or observing the subject, write your findings in a notebook. Date each entry and describe your method of observation.

5. Outline your report. Your outline should list the main points that you want to write about in the order you want to present them. Usually, you will begin with an introduction that briefly states the question you wanted to answer and the answer that you found.

6. Draft your report. Present the information in clear, concise prose. In the text, or in a list attached to your paper, tell where you found each fact. End with a summary that helps readers understand the information that you presented.

7. Edit your draft. Check it for accuracy and clarity.

8. Test the report with a trial reader. Ask for feedback. Then revise your report if you find ways to improve it.

Activity Extensions

The following ideas are meant to enrich the lessons, either by suggesting additional topics or different media, for example, having the teacher do an activity which the students describe.

Comparing and Contrasting
In language arts, students write reviews that compare and contrast:
• two nonfiction books on the same subject
• two novels by the same author
• two films of the same genre (science fiction, comedy, thriller)
• two television news shows from different channels
• two sitcoms
• two paintings by the same painter
In social studies, students write essays that compare and contrast:
• two cities
• two centuries
• the impact of two inventions (telephone/TV; airplane/railroad)
• leadership of the prime minister in a parliamentary system and leadership of the president in a U.S. style form of government

Comparing: Making an Analogy
In science, students write reports that compare different structures used for the same purpose:
• bird's wings and human feet (both used for locomotion)
• photography film and light-sensitive cells in the human eye
• termite society and human society
• spread of computer virus and spread of a human virus

Condensing an Article (and other kinds of writing)
• Students take turn condensing the day's top news story.
• Students condense the material in a textbook or the lessons covered each week in each curriculum area. These reports can be shared with parents to keep them up to date.
• Students compress published biographies into 100-word reports.
• Students sum up the plot of a half-hour sitcom in 100 words.

Descriptive Writing
• Regularly have students translate pictures from postcards, magazines, or other sources into word pictures.
• Have students write descriptive passages and ask partners to make drawings based on the text.

Descriptive Writing: Actions

• Play a video of a movie scene or a commercial, and have students translate the action into words.

• Have a student (perhaps an actor from your local high school) mime actions while students observe and then describe them.

• Demonstrate a skill—such as drawing, folding origami, or juggling—and have the students describe it.

Descriptive Writing: Analysis

• Show students antique tools (churn, farm implement) and let students describe the objects in detail and then speculate on their uses. (Photographs from a book about antiques will work well.)

• Magnified views: Students observe objects using a magnifying glass or microscope and describe what they see in detail.

• Tactile reports: Place an object in a bag. Have students feel it and describe it in detail. Possible objects include: chess piece, children's wood block with raised letters, combination lock, paper clip, pencil (unsharpened), sock, tennis ball, and walnut. Students will usually recognize the object, but that doesn't matter as long as the details they report must come from touching.

Descriptive Writing: Groups

Have students distinguish between items in a set, for example: two sweet potatoes, two walnuts, or two bananas.

Descriptive Writing: Sounds

• Make a short audio recording of sounds in your neighborhood or in a place with lots of activities. Play the tape for the class and have them describe the place and the sounds.

• Read aloud poetry that contains sound images. Then have students write their own poems on different subjects. Here's an example from "Casey at the Bat":

> Then from five thousand throats and more there rose a lusty yell;
> It rumbled through the valley, it rattled in the dell
> It pounded on the mountain and recoiled upon the flat,
> For Casey, mighty Casey, was advancing to the bat.

Descriptive Writing: Zoom In

Cut small squares in the middle of sheets of plain paper. Then have students use the "windows" to zoom in on details in pictures.

Elaborating Fiction

- Students can turn three-panel comics into stories.
- Students can rewrite jokes as stories. Take the classic: *What did one wall say to the other wall? "I'll meet you at the corner."* Add a little imagination, and you get the makings of a novel:

> I'm a wall. People say that I'm nice looking. I suppose they're referring to the paper that covers me. It has pictures of airplanes, from the Wright Brothers' first model to jets.
>
> Still I'm extremely shy. I might be the shyest wall you ever met. The other day I looked up and saw another wall staring at me. The wall wore the same outfit as I did. I thought maybe we could be friends. Unfortunately, the other wall said nothing. Maybe it was shy like me. I took a breath and said, "Would you like to talk?"
>
> Immediately, the other wall smiled and said, "Sure."
>
> "Where should we get together?" I asked.
>
> The other wall thought for a second, and then said, "Why don't you meet me at the corner."

Elaborating Nonfiction

Have students describe a personal experience, such as going to the dentist or taking a trip. Limit the description to a few words, for example, 50. A day or so later, ask students to expand the piece by two or three times, using the original but adding details.

Explaining Behavior

Have students explain the behavior of characters in fables, movies, or books that they have read. For example, the following paragraph gives one person's theory about why, in Aesop's "The Ant and the Grasshopper," the ant didn't feed the grasshopper:

> Some people might say that the ant was being selfish by not sharing what it had. However, I think the ant was actually helping the grasshopper. If the ant had given the grasshopper food, the grasshopper would not have learned to take responsibility. True, the grasshopper will be hungry now, but that hunger may teach it a lesson. If the next summer, the grasshopper changes its behavior, it will have a much better life than if it was always begging someone for food.

Other topics include:
- Why did the father in Rumpelstiltskin say that his daughter could spin straw into gold?
- Why did Jack climb the beanstalk?
- Why did Cinderella's stepsisters treat her meanly?

Explaining with Diagrams
Students can draw floor plans of the classroom or a room at home, and label the parts to what goes on in that place.

Explaining with Examples
When students write book reviews, have them include excerpts that support their generalizations. For example, after stating that a book is exciting, a student should excerpt an exciting scene.

Humor: Using Exaggeration
• Parodies of commercials often feature exaggeration: "Sun-Brite Toothpaste will make your teeth so shiny, you'll need sunglasses when you look in a mirror. When reading at night, you won't need to turn on a lamp. Just smile and your teeth will light the page."
• Humorous fantasies, such as *Alice's Adventures in Wonderland*, often involve an exaggerated use of detail. Here's an example:

A snake went into a clothing shop. It was one of the fancy boutiques on Third Street just off Willow, the kind that appeal to wealthy woman, and that was fine because the snake was a female, an Eastern diamond by the way.

Two clerks were standing behind the counter, chatting, with obviously nothing to do. As the snake examined shirts, sweaters, blouses, and dresses, from time to time, she tried to make eye contact with the clerks. Nothing came of it. Eventually, the snake shook her rattle, which was made up of horny plates. You might have guessed that the high-pitched buzz would have got the clerks' attention. But...

Humor: Using Puns
Beyond fun, punning raises awareness of homonyms, which are a major cause of spelling errors. In addition to writing punning jokes, students might create punning riddles ("puniddles"): a question answered by a pair of homonyms in the form of a phrase or a sentence. Two examples:

What do you call a story about the end a dog? A tail tale.
What warning did the mother insect shout when the cat began to scratch? Flee, flea!

More homonym pairs to use:

ant/aunt	hear/here	pail/pale
ate/eight	heard/herd	side/sighed
blew/blue	heal/heel	sight/site
fair/fare	mail/male	toe/tow

Interpreting Proverbs

• More proverbs to interpret:

The early bird catches the worm.
Don't judge a book by its cover.
Birds of a feather flock together.
One rotten apple spoils the barrel.
The grass is always greener on the
   other side of the fence.
You made your bed, now lie in it.
The leopard can't change his spots.
Half a loaf is better than none.
When the cat's away, the mice
   will play.
A stitch in time saves nine.
The squeaky wheel gets the
   grease.
Don't cross your bridges until you
   come to them.
A small hole can sink a large ship.
Love me, love my dog.
Don't change horses in mid-stream.

In the kingdom of the blind men, the
   one-eyed man is king.
Let sleeping dogs lie.
You reap what you sow.
Where there's smoke, there's fire.
He who cannot dance will say:
   "The drum is bad."
All sunshine makes a desert.
The journey of a thousand miles
   begins with a single step.
Drop by drop fills the tub.
Many take by the bushel and give
   by the spoon.
A net does not make a fisherman.
Yesterday's storm causes no
   damage today.
Measure your cloth 10 times, you
   can cut it only once.
You can't learn to swim in a field.

• In addition to interpreting proverbs, challenge students to explain the
meaning of short poems, such as haiku, or excerpts from longer poems.
Here's an example from William Blake's "The Fly":

   Little Fly,
   Thy summer's play
   My thoughtless hand
   Has brushed away.

   Am not I
   A fly like thee?
   Or art not thou
   A man like me?

   For I dance
   And drink and sing,
   Till some blind hand
   Shall brush my wing.

• Have students interpret visual works, both classics, such as Leonardo da
Vinci's "Mona Lisa," and modern works, copies of which are often on loan
at public libraries.

Memory Writing
• Read aloud an essay or a short story. Then, a few days later, ask students to write the work from memory. The goal should be to replicate the work as accurately as possible, and not merely to summarize it. Afterwards, read the essay or story again.
• Play a scene from a movie. A few days later, ask students to describe the scene from memory. Afterwards, show the scene again.
• Present a work of art. A few days later, ask students to describe it from memory. Then let the students observe the work.

Naming Things
More things to rename:
• Animals: bird, camel, cat, dinosaur, dog, mosquito, shark, skunk, whale
• Clothing: belt, gloves, jacket, scarf
• Foods: ice cream, mashed potatoes, pizza, sandwich, spaghetti
• Games: checkers, chess, hopscotch, tag
• Household appliances: microwave oven, refrigerator, stove, vacuum cleaner, washing machine
• Inventions: computer, laser, rocket, telephone
• Sports: baseball, basketball, hockey, soccer
• Vehicles: airplane, automobile, boat, subway, train, truck

Paraphrasing
Have students practice paraphrasing newspaper stories, novels (chapters or scenes), or textbook chapters.

Personification
• In science, have students use personification to give information about objects such as a bacterium, a cell, an earthquake, an electron, a light wave, and a planet.
• In language arts, have students give oral reports in which they personify linguistic topics such as parts of speech, types of sentences, tenses, and writing tools (dictionary, thesaurus, word processor).

Persuasive Writing
Have students write letters to the editor urging readers to adopt positions on subjects of community interest, for example, installing bicycle lanes or increasing support of the library.

Point of View
Regularly have students translate stories from one point of view to another. For example, after reading a short story written in the third person, students could rewrite it in the first or second person.

Pros and Cons

Students debate the pros and cons of various issues, such as:
- giving the vote to elementary or junior high students
- making schooling voluntary
- granting animals the same rights as people
- extending the school year by 25%

Questioning

- Arrange for students in an earlier grade to send questions to your students, who will then respond with answers.
- Try the same activity with your students writing the questions to be answered by students in a high school or college class.
- Each week have a different student (or small group) post a question of the week on a bulletin board (in a hallway or on a Web site).

Ranking

Students write research papers structured by ranking. Possible topics are:
- the five longest rivers in the world
- the five most important inventions
- the five most memorable natural disasters
- the five most exciting sporting events
- the five meanest villains in literature

Scientific Reporting

- While students observe objects through a magnifying glass or a microscope, they should draw what they see, and then write detailed descriptions.
- Students observe a changing subject at regular intervals, and write detailed reports on what they see. Possible subjects are: a seed growing, the moon waxing and waning, water freezing or unfreezing, and a banana ripening.

Scripting

Have students write scripts based on well-known children's books, such as *The Runaway Bunny* or *Where the Wild Things Are*. Later, the students could perform the scripts—live or as puppet plays—for younger children.

Sentence Linking

Divide students into small groups. Each student writes a sentence of at least five words. Students exchange papers. Each adds a sentence that links the first. The activity continues for a set time or set number of sentences. This can also be done orally.

Simplifying
Students simplify material from a textbook or a newspaper, aiming it for a child in an earlier grade. If possible, the simplified versions should be tested with the younger students.

Speculative Writing
Students write science fiction stories based on speculations from the prompt cards.

Storytelling: Character Combining
Students create characters based on people that they know, for example, creating a private detective who has a friend's brilliance in mathematics with a cousin's sports skills. Students can then write stories based on their characters.

Storytelling: Dialogue
• Cover up the dialogue in a comic strip or comic book, and have students write new dialogue for the images.
• Challenge students to write entirely new dialogue for a familiar fairy tale, or for an excerpt from a novel.

Storytelling: Endings
• Students write new endings for familiar stories.
• Students think up dramatic endings, and then exchange them with classmates who write stories leading to the endings.

Storytelling: Finding Plots
Students find newspaper articles and turn them into short stories. The obituary section is an especially rich source of material.

Storytelling: Recycled Plots
Students twist famous movie plots into new stories. For example, in a new version of *Jaws*, the shark becomes someone's pet fish.

Summarizing a Story
• Students summarize novels in 100 words.
• Students summarize movies in 100 words.
• Students summarize their lives, or the lives of other people in 100 words.

Titling a Piece of Writing
When students write an original essay or story, have them submit three possible titles, choose one, and explain the choice.

Practice Log

Each time you finish a writing prompt, put the date in the space after the title below. If you do more than one practice for a type of writing, date each practice. For example, you might have three dates in the "Describing Writing: Actions" category.

Comparing and Contrasting _____

Comparing: Analogies _____

Condensing an Article _____

Descriptive Writing _____

Descriptive Writing: Actions _____

Descriptive Writing: Analysis _____

Descriptive Writing: Groups _____

Descriptive Writing: Sounds _____

Descriptive Writing: Zoom In _____

Elaborating Fiction _____

Elaborating Nonfiction _____

Explaining Behavior _____

Explaining with Diagrams _____

Explaining with Examples _____

Humor: Using Exaggeration _____

Humor: Using Puns _____

Interpreting Proverbs _____

Memory Writing: Objects _____

Memory Writing: People _____

Naming Things _____

Practice Log (continued)

Paraphrasing _____

Personification _____

Persuasive Writing _____

Point of View: First Person _____

Point of View: Second Person _____

Point of View: Third Person _____

Pros and Cons _____

Questioning _____

Ranking _____

Science Observation _____

Scripting an Adaptation _____

Scripting a Commercial _____

Sentence Linking _____

Simplifying _____

Speculative Writing _____

Storytelling: Characters _____

Storytelling: Dialogue _____

Storytelling: Endings _____

Storytelling: Finding Plots _____

Storytelling: Recycled Plots _____

Summarizing a Story _____

Titling a Piece of Writing _____

Index